2

MILITARY AND VETERAN ISSUES

SUPPORT FOR SERVICEMEMBERS AND VETERANS

PROGRAMS ADDRESSING THE EFFECTS OF COMBAT AND TRANSITION TO CIVILIAN LIFE

MILITARY AND VETERAN ISSUES

Additional books in this series can be found on Nova's website under the Series tab.

Additional e-books in this series can be found on Nova's website under the e-book tab.

MILITARY AND VETERAN ISSUES

SUPPORT FOR SERVICEMEMBERS AND VETERANS

PROGRAMS ADDRESSING THE EFFECTS OF COMBAT AND TRANSITION TO CIVILIAN LIFE

GAYLE MARSH
EDITOR

New York

Library of Congress Cataloging-in-Publication Data

ISBN: 978-1-63484-950-0

Published by Nova Science Publishers, Inc. † New York

CONTENTS

PREFACE

The Department of Defense (DOD) and the Department of Veterans Affairs (VA) play key roles in offering post-combat support to servicemembers and veterans through various programs and activities. This book identifies the number of programs, including the types of services offered that address the effects of combat on post-9/11 active-duty servicemembers and their families; help post-9/11 servicemembers and veterans transition to civilian life; and help raise public awareness and understanding of servicemembers' and veterans' combat and transition experiences.

In: Support for Servicemembers and Veterans ISBN: 978-1-63484-950-0
Editor: Gayle Marsh

Chapter 1

MILITARY AND VETERAN SUPPORT: DOD AND VA PROGRAMS THAT ADDRESS THE EFFECTS OF COMBAT AND TRANSITION TO CIVILIAN LIFE*

United States Government Accountability Office

WHY GAO DID THIS STUDY

DOD and VA play key roles in offering post-combat support to servicemembers and veterans through various programs and activities. Congress mandated that GAO identify DOD and VA programs designed to address the effects of combat on servicemembers who have served during recent conflicts, assist servicemembers and veterans with the transition to civilian life, and raise public awareness of these issues.

In this report GAO identified the number of programs, including the types of services offered that: 1) address the effects of combat on post-9/11 active-duty servicemembers and their families, 2) help post-9/11 servicemembers and veterans transition to civilian life, and 3) help raise public awareness and understanding of servicemembers' and veterans' combat and transition experiences. Also, GAO examined how the lists of programs identified compare with program inventories prepared by DOD and VA pursuant to law.

---

* This is an edited, reformatted and augmented version of the United States Government Accountability Office publication, GAO-15-24, dated November 2014.

To address these objectives, GAO established and applied its definition of "program." In general, GAO defined programs as federally funded, organized sets of activities agencies undertake that are directed toward specific purposes or goals and are being administered in fiscal year 2014. GAO also searched publicly available sources that contain lists of programs; sent preliminary lists of programs to DOD and VA for verification; and reviewed relevant reports and 2013 program inventories for DOD and VA.

This report contains no recommendations.

WHAT GAO FOUND

GAO identified 99 programs provided by the Department of Defense (DOD) to help address the effects of combat on post-9/11 servicemembers, their families, or both. These programs often offer multiple types of services. The services most common are mental health and substance abuse (50), information and referral (37), and case management or care coordination (15).

GAO identified 87 programs administered either by DOD or the Department of Veterans Affairs (VA) to help post-9/11 servicemembers and veterans transition to civilian life. Some of the 87 programs offer more than one type of service, such as the Transition Assistance Program, which offers employment, education, and information on veterans' benefits, among other services.

GAO identified 12 programs administered by either DOD or VA to raise public awareness and understanding of servicemembers' and veterans' experiences in combat, coming home, and transitioning to civilian life. For example, among the nine DOD programs identified, the Briefings with the Boss program convenes employers and National Guard and Reserve members to discuss issues linked to military service and civilian employment.

The lists of programs that GAO developed using its definition are not comparable with those in DOD's 2013 program inventory and have only limited comparability with VA's 2013 program inventory. This limited comparability is primarily due to differing contexts in which the lists were compiled. While GAO's lists address specific mandated questions, DOD's and VA's lists were developed following Office of Management and Budget guidance, which generally provides flexibility in how agencies define their programs. Both DOD and VA chose to identify programs at a broad level. For example, DOD's inventory is partially organized by its strategic goals. One goal is "preserving and enhancing the all-volunteer force," for which wounded warrior care is cited as a high priority. Under this goal, DOD lists "hospitals" and "regional defense facilities" as programs. In contrast, GAO identified individual programs, such as the Army Wounded Warrior Program and Warrior Transition Units, which were not listed in DOD's inventory.

ABBREVIATIONS

CFDA	Catalog of Federal Domestic Assistance
DOD	U.S. Department of Defense
GPRAMA	GPRA Modernization Act of 2010
IC3	Interagency Care Coordination Committee
IDES	Integrated Disability Evaluation System
OEF/OIF/OND	Operation Enduring Freedom, Operation Iraqi Freedom, and Operation New Dawn
OMB	Office of Management and Budget
Post-9/11 GI Bill	Post-9/11 Veterans Educational Assistance Act of 2008
PTSD	Posttraumatic stress disorder
TAP	Transition Assistance Program
TBI	Traumatic Brain Injury
VA	U.S. Department of Veterans Affairs

***

November 7, 2014

Congressional Committees

To help meet the needs of post-9/11 servicemembers, veterans, and their families, various federal agencies administer a number of programs, many of which may experience increased demand following more than a decade of war and as the United States military looks toward reducing the overall size of its forces. After they leave the military, some veterans' readjustment to civilian life will go smoothly, while others may struggle with health problems related to their service, employment, and relationships.[1] In addition, researchers, media outlets, and others have reported on a gap in public awareness and understanding of the challenges many post-9/11 veterans face while transitioning from the military to civilian life.

The Department of Defense (DOD) and the Department of Veterans Affairs (VA) play key roles in offering various types of post-combat assistance to servicemembers and veterans. DOD offers, among other things, (1) care to wounded and injured servicemembers during their recovery, (2) mental health counseling and suicide prevention efforts, (3) support for military families, and (4) assistance to servicemembers who are transitioning out of the military. VA offers veterans a wide variety of benefits and services, including health care, counseling, education, housing, employment-related services, and disability compensation benefits.

To instill a more coordinated and crosscutting perspective to federal performance, among other aims, the GPRA Modernization Act of 2010 (GPRAMA) was enacted.[2] GPRAMA requires that (1) the Office of Management and Budget (OMB) coordinate with federal agencies to develop federal government priority goals, including outcome-oriented goals covering a limited number of cross-cutting policy areas; (2) federal agencies, in developing their own performance plans, describe how they will work with other agencies to achieve their performance goals; and, (3) OMB make publicly available a list of all federal programs identified by agencies, including information about the purposes of each program, how it contributes to the agency's mission, and recent funding information. OMB published the lists of programs—referred to as program inventories—developed by 24 federal agencies, including DOD and VA, in May 2013.[3]

Apart from the GPRAMA inventories, Congress mandated that we provide a comprehensive list of DOD and VA programs that address a range of challenges that servicemembers and veterans who have served during recent conflicts may face.[4] This report identifies:

1. the number of DOD programs addressing the effects of combat on post-9/11 active-duty servicemembers and their families,
2. the number of DOD and VA programs to help post-9/11 active-duty servicemembers transition and veterans readjust to civilian life, and
3. the number of DOD and VA programs to help raise public awareness and understanding of post-9/11 active-duty servicemembers' and veterans' combat and readjustment experiences.

In addition, in light of our prior work, we examined:

4.how the lists of programs identified by GAO compare with program inventories prepared by DOD and VA pursuant to the GPRA Modernization Act of 2010.[5]

This report also provides a description of the types of services provided by the programs identified in objectives 1-2.

To address objectives 1-3, we identified DOD and VA programs through the following four-step process:

(1) We established a definition for "program" by reviewing our prior work and other relevant studies on related programs for servicemembers and veterans who have served in recent conflicts.[6] We also obtained input from our internal (GAO) experts as well as officials from DOD and VA. In general, we defined programs as federally funded, organized sets of activities directed toward specific purposes or goals that agencies undertake and are being administered in fiscal year 2014.[7] Given this definition, we included activities that were not formally labeled as a program, such as the Integrated Disability Evaluation System (IDES) and the Mobile Vet Centers.[8] We further scoped this definition for each objective as follows:[9]

- Objective 1: DOD or military services' programs that address the effects of combat—including physical, mental, or social heath—on post-9/11 active-duty servicemembers or their spouses or dependents.
- Objective 2: DOD, military services, or VA programs that focus primarily on helping active duty servicemembers transition or veterans readjust to civilian life.
- Objective 3: DOD, military services, or VA programs that focus primarily on raising civilian public awareness of the combat experiences of servicemembers and the readjustment experiences of veterans.

(We further elaborate on these definitions in appendix I.[10])

(2) We identified publicly available sources that contain lists of relevant programs, such as the National Resource Directory and Catalog of Federal Domestic Assistance (CFDA).[11] We identified these sources based on discussions with DOD and VA officials and internal GAO experts as well as through online searches. (See app. I for a description of the sources we used.)

(3) We used the definitions and sources from steps 1 and 2 to review and identify the relevant programs for our lists.

(4) We sent our preliminary lists of programs to officials at DOD and VA for comment and verification, and we modified the lists accordingly.[12]

This four-step process identified 170 separate programs, although some of them are relevant to more than one objective. Specifically, 26 programs are included in more than one objective, such as the Air Force Wounded Warrior Program (AFW2) that addresses the effects of combat and helps wounded and injured servicemembers transition to civilian life. In addition, to present our results, we developed categories to group the types of services provided by the programs. Because some programs offer more than one type of service, programs can fall into more than one category or service type.[13]

We did not analyze these DOD and VA programs to identify any instances of fragmentation, overlap, duplication, or gaps in benefits or services. Our scope for the first three objectives was limited to identifying DOD and VA programs based on the types of service provided. In addition, in carrying out this four-step process, we did not conduct an independent legal analysis of the statutory or regulatory basis or requirements for any of the programs we identified.

To address the fourth objective, we compared the lists of programs that we generated under objectives 1-3 with DOD and VA's 2013 GPRAMA program inventories to identify similarities and differences between the agencies' inventories and our lists. Also, we drew upon our prior work on agencies' GPRAMA program inventories.[14]

We conducted our work from March 2014 to November 2014 in accordance with generally accepted government auditing standards. Those standards require that we plan and perform the audit to obtain sufficient, appropriate evidence to provide a reasonable basis for our findings and conclusions based on our audit objectives. We believe that the evidence obtained provides a reasonable basis for our findings based on our audit objectives.

BACKGROUND

During the last decade of U.S. military operations, servicemembers have experienced numerous deployments, which increase the risk for posttraumatic stress disorder (PTSD) and traumatic brain injury (TBI), two common conditions that many post-9/11 servicemembers and veterans suffer.[15] Additionally, more seriously wounded servicemembers survive their injuries—injuries that in previous wars would have been fatal—given improvements to body armor and military medicine, but may be left with significant disabilities.

Less than 1 percent of the American population has served on active duty in an all-volunteer, professional military—an historic low—resulting in a so-called "military-civilian" gap. While Americans generally hold the military in high regard, there is a reported lack of awareness and understanding of the difficult challenges many post-9/11 servicemembers have faced while transitioning from the military to civilian life.[16]

Federal Assistance to Servicemembers, Veterans, and Their Families

DOD and VA play key roles in offering assistance to servicemembers, veterans, and their families. In particular, DOD has a role in preparing servicemembers, including those who have served from 9/11 onward, for careers beyond the military and helping them transition from active duty to veteran status. After servicemembers separate from the military, VA's role is generally to help veterans readjust to civilian life. VA provides health care and other benefits to veterans who have served in all conflicts and wars, such as World War II; Vietnam; and Operation Enduring Freedom, Operation Iraqi Freedom, and Operation New Dawn or OEF/OIF/OND.

DOD and VA have coordinated in assisting servicemembers and veterans and have jointly developed and implemented policies for the care, management, and transition of recovering servicemembers. These policies address certain issues such as care coordination and the disability evaluation process. In a subsequent but related effort, in May 2012, a joint entity known as the DOD/VA Warrior Care & Coordination Task Force began an inventory of DOD and VA programs and established the Interagency Care Coordination Committee (IC3) to guide the development of shared care coordination policies and practices. Additionally, DOD, VA and other agency partners administer the Transition Assistance Program (TAP), which provides counseling to departing servicemembers, and offers employment assistance and information on federal veteran benefits, among other things.[17] VA refers to the revised TAP as Transition, Goals, Plans, Success (Transition GPS).

Our past reports, as well as reports by others, have highlighted issues surrounding DOD and VA programs, including issues concerning fragmentation, overlap, and duplication; lack of coordination; and challenges in providing some benefits and services.[18] For example, we have recommended in two GAO reports that DOD and VA need to better integrate care coordination and case management programs to reduce duplication and better assist recovering servicemembers, veterans, and their families by helping to ensure the continuity of their care. In response, a joint DOD-VA council approved the implementation of specific initiatives that are intended to improve care coordination procedures by facilitating communication between departments and eliminating duplicative efforts. As of September 2014, the departments had not fully implemented these initiatives, according to a senior DOD official. As previously noted, this report does not address fragmentation, overlap, and duplication in benefits or services.

Other federal agencies also offer assistance to servicemembers and veterans and bring to bear a variety of policy tools. For example, as we have previously reported, the Department of Labor administers four employment programs targeted to veterans.[19] In addition, the Department of Housing and Urban Development provides permanent housing and case management for eligible homeless veterans; and the Internal Revenue Service administers tax expenditures, such as tax credits for businesses hiring veterans, as well as other special tax benefits.

GPRA Modernization Act and Agency Coordination

With various federal programs spread across multiple federal agencies, concerns have been raised that no full accounting of the breadth and effectiveness of these programs exists. Among its aims, GPRAMA seeks to instill a more coordinated and crosscutting perspective to federal performance; that is, improving connections across organizations and policy tools. As we have noted in our past work and OMB states in its guidance, effective implementation of GPRAMA could play an important role in clarifying desired outcomes, addressing program performance spanning multiple organizations, and facilitating future actions to reduce duplication, overlap, and fragmentation.[20] Some of the GPRAMA requirements and related OMB guidance that emphasize collaboration include:

- **Federal government priority goals:** GPRAMA requires OMB to coordinate with agencies to establish federal government priority goals that include outcome-oriented goals covering a limited number of policy areas, as well as goals for needed management improvements across the government.
- **Agency priority goals:** Certain agencies are required by GPRAMA to identify from among their performance goals a limited number of

priority goals every 2 years. Each agency's priority goals are to reflect the agency's highest priorities, as identified by the head of the agency, and be informed by the federal government priority goals, as well as input from relevant congressional committees.[21]

- **Agency performance plans:** Agencies' performance plans are required to describe how the performance goals (including priority goals) are to be achieved, including a description of how the agency is working with other agencies to achieve its performance goals.
- **Strategic reviews:** In its 2012 guidance (and subsequent updates) for implementing GPRAMA, OMB guidance directs agencies to conduct annual strategic reviews of progress toward strategic objectives to inform their decision making, beginning in 2014.[22] Agency leaders are responsible for assessing progress on each strategic objective established in the agency strategic plan, including mission, as well as management or crosscutting objectives. Among other things, the reviews are intended to strengthen collaboration on crosscutting issues by identifying and addressing crosscutting challenges or fragmentation.
- **Federal program inventory:** As previously noted, GPRAMA requires OMB to make publicly available a list of all federal programs identified by agencies, and to include the purposes of each program, how it contributes to the agency's mission and goals, and recent funding information. GPRAMA also requires OMB to issue guidance to ensure that this information presents a coherent picture of all federal programs. OMB is taking a phased approach to implement this provision and published the inventories developed by 24 agencies in May 2013.

We Identified 99 DOD Programs That Address the Effects of Combat

Using our definition of "program," we identified 99 healthcare and benefit programs administered by DOD and the military services that address the effects of combat on servicemembers, their families, or both. Some of these 99 programs we identified share a common name, but are independently implemented by each branch of the military service. For example, each military service administers wounded warrior programs. These programs provide care coordination for recovering servicemembers and their families as they transition to and readjust to civilian life. This population includes servicemembers and veterans who suffer from TBI, amputations, burns, spinal cord injuries, visual impairment, and PTSD. Over a third of the 99 programs that we identified offer multiple types of services. A sample of programs we identified is contained in table 1, which we categorize by type of service to illustrate the range of services provided. The full array of programs is listed in appendix II. In addition, a detailed, interactive list of programs is available at http://www.gao.gov/products/GAO-15-24.

Table 1. Selected DOD Programs Addressing the Effects of Combat

Program	Type of Service	Program Description	Agency
Air Force Wounded Warrior Program (AFW2)	Case management/care coordination	Coordinates care to servicemembers from the point of injury, through separation or retirement, for life. The program provides a range of services, such as transition, employment, and moving assistance as well as financial counseling; and seeks to integrate servicemembers and their families into their local communities. The program also coordinates benefits provided by other agencies.	DOD - Air Force
Combat and Operational Stress Control Program	Mental health and substance abuse	Provides content and resources to help Army soldiers, leaders, and family members endure the stress of combat and military operations.	DOD - Army
Command Suicide Prevention Program	Mental health and substance abuse	Provides training to increase awareness of suicide concerns, improve wellness, and techniques that could be used to intervene when someone needs help and assistance to families and servicemembers affected by suicidal behaviors.	DOD – Navy

Program	Type of Service	Program Description	Agency
Computer/Electronic Accommodations Program (CAP)	Disability	Provides assistive technology and reasonable accommodations to servicemembers and veterans with disabilities who work at DOD and other federal agencies.	DOD
Joint Family Support Assistance Program (JFSAP)	Counseling; Information and referral	Provides support for families who are far from a military installation, working with National Guard and reserve military and family programs to augment existing family programs. Service providers offer information on military programs, military partnerships in the civilian community and short-term, confidential non-medical counseling to individuals, couples and families.	DOD
Marine Forces Reserve (MARFORRES) Chaplain	Spiritual health	Provides for the free exercise of religion by all servicemembers and provides ministry that helps enhance the moral, personal, and spiritual growth of servicemembers. Counseling of servicemembers' dependents is also provided.	DOD – Marine Corps
Military Adaptive Sports Program (MASP)	Physical health; Disability	Enhances recovery by engaging ill, injured, and wounded servicemembers in individualized physical and cognitive activities and competitive athletics outside of traditional therapy settings, inspiring recovery, physical fitness, and encouraging new opportunities for growth and achievement.	DOD

Program	Type of Service	Program Description	Agency
Operation: Military Kids (OMK)	Information and referral	Connects military children and youth with local resources to help achieve a sense of community support and enhance their well-being. OMK objectives are to raise community awareness and understanding about how deployment affects military children and to provide education and training to community organizations to better support military children.	DOD - Army
Special Compensation for Assistance with Activities of Daily Living (SCAADL)	Caregiver support; Disability	Helps offset the loss of income by a primary caregiver who provides non-medical care, support, and assistance for the servicemember. This special monthly compensation is for servicemembers who incur a catastrophic injury or illness.	DOD –all military services
Wounded Soldier and Family Hotline	Information and referral	Offers recovering servicemembers and their families a way to share concerns on the quality of patient care. The hotline is used to gather information about medical care as well as suggest ways to improve medical support systems.	DOD - Army

Source: GAO analysis of Department of Defense (DOD) and Department of Veterans Affairs (VA) programs. | GAO-15-24

Note: Some of these 99 programs we identified share a common name but are independently implemented by each service branch of the military, such as the Wounded Warrior Program. In these instances, we separately counted each military service's program.

The three services most common in the 99 programs are support for mental health and substance abuse (50), information and referral (37), and case management or care coordination (15). The number and types of services in the DOD programs are presented in figure 1.[23]

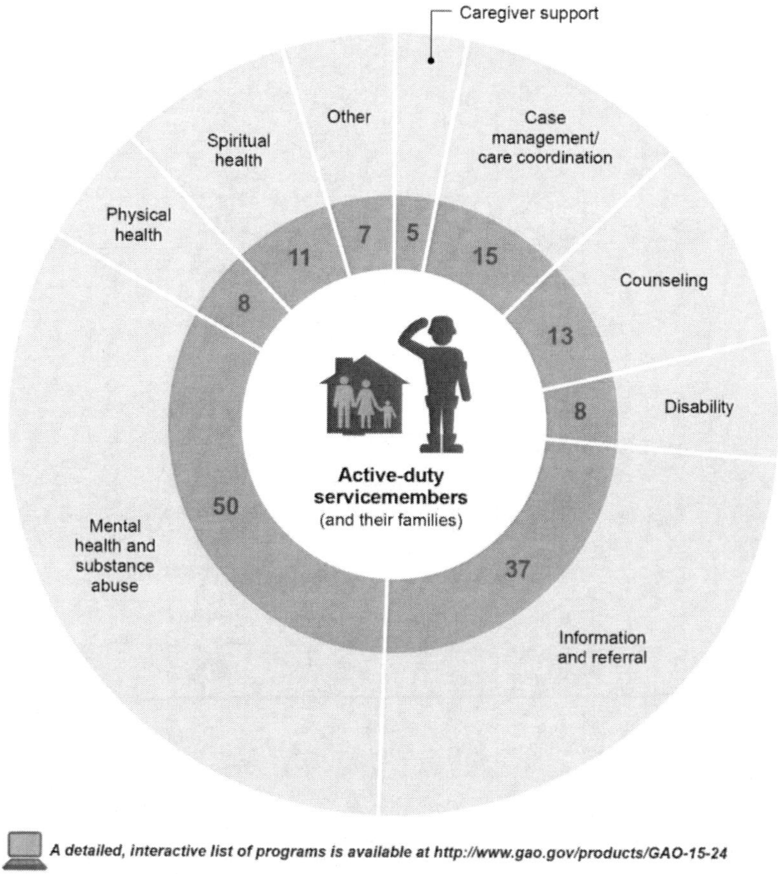

Source GAO analysis of Department of Defence (DOD) and Department of Veterans Affairs (VA) programs. | GAO-15-24

Notes: Numbers of services do not add up to 99 because some programs provide more than one type of service. In addition, under type of service, the "Spiritual health" category includes services such as religious ministry, pastoral care, and counseling. For example, the Strong Bonds program provides chaplain-sponsored couple and family events to help servicemembers reconnect with family after deployments. The frequency of a type of service does not necessarily indicate its utilization.

A detailed, interactive list of programs is available at http://www.gao.gov/ products/GAO-15-24.

Figure 1. Addressing the Effects of Combat: Number of DOD Programs by Type of Service.

Table 2. Selected DOD and VA Programs for Transitioning and Readjusting to Civilian Life

Program	Type of Service	Program Description	Agency
Clothing Allowance	Disability	Provides clothing allowances to veterans with service-connected disabilities who use prosthetic or orthopedic appliances which tend to wear or tear clothing, and to veterans who use a prescribed medication for a skin condition (due to a service-connected disability) that irreparably damages outer garments.	VA – Veterans Health Administration (VHA)
Coaching Into Care	Caregiver support	Provides a free and confidential coaching service to friends and family members of veterans to help them learn new ways to talk about their concerns and ways to motivate veterans to seek assistance.	VA
Federal Recovery Coordination Program	Case management/care coordination	Provides care coordination by tracking care, management and transition of a recovering servicemember or veteran through recovery, rehabilitation, and reintegration.	DOD and VA
in Transition	Information and referral; Mental health and substance abuse	Provides information and referrals to servicemembers receiving mental health treatment. Specifically, this program aims to ease the transition between health care systems and providers.	DOD – Defense Centers of Excellence (DCoE) for Psychological Health & Traumatic Brain Injury and VA
Job Fairs	Employment assistance	Promotes the employment of members of the National Guard and Reserves by hosting and sending representatives to attend job fairs and by maintaining a website.	DOD – Employer Support of the Guard and Reserve (ESGR)
Navy Returning Warrior Workshop	Counseling	Provides workshops to servicemembers and their families to teach them how to overcome struggles that come from the dramatic transition from combat life to civilian life. Workshops are comprised of group presentations, small group breakout sessions, vendor informational sessions, and one-on-one counseling in a conference-style setting.	DOD - Navy

Program	Type of Service	Program Description	Agency
Post-9/11 GI Bill	Education assistance	Provides post-secondary education benefits for individuals with active-duty service after September 10, 2001, or individuals discharged with a service-connected disability after 30 days. Benefits can be used for a range of learning programs, including undergraduate and graduate degrees, non-college degree programs, and apprenticeship and on-the-job training. Some servicemembers can transfer their benefits to dependents.	VA –Veterans Benefit Administration (VBA)
Spinal Cord Injury and Disorders Centers	Disability; Physical health	Provides veterans with spinal cord injury with specialized rehabilitative services at one of the 24 Spinal Cord Injury Centers available through VA.	VA - VHA
Temporary Residence Adaptation (TRA)	Disability; Other (Housing)	Provides grants to eligible veterans and servicemembers who are temporarily residing in a home owned by a family member to help adapt the home to meet his or her special needs.	VA - VBA
Yellow Ribbon Reintegration Programs	Information and referral	Helps servicemembers and their families connect with local resources before, during, and after deployments. Provides information, referrals, and outreach.	DOD – Army, Navy, Air Force, Marine Corps

Source: GAO analysis of Department of Defense (DOD) and Department of Veterans Affairs (VA) programs. | GAO-15-24.

In addition, for 73 of the 99 programs (about 75 percent), a servicemember's or veteran's family is also eligible for the services or benefits provided. Also, one of these 99 programs—the Federal Recovery Coordination Program—is jointly administered by DOD and VA.

WE IDENTIFIED 87 DOD AND VA PROGRAMS THAT HELP SERVICEMEMBERS TRANSITION AND VETERANS READJUST TO CIVILIAN LIFE

Using our definition of "program," we identified 87 programs administered by DOD and VA that help servicemembers transition and veterans readjust to civilian life. Some of these programs share a common name, but are independently implemented through their respective military service branch, such as the Yellow Ribbon Reintegration Program. As a result, we separately counted each military service's program. A sample of the programs we identified is contained in Table 2, which we categorize by type of service. The full array of programs is listed in appendix III. In addition, a detailed, interactive list of programs is available at http://www.gao.gov/ products/GAO-15-24.

The three services most common in the 87 programs are disability benefits or services (19); employment assistance (18); and, case management/care coordination, counseling, information and referral, as well as physical health (the frequency for these types of services is 16). The frequency and types of service offered across these 87 programs are portrayed in Figure 2.

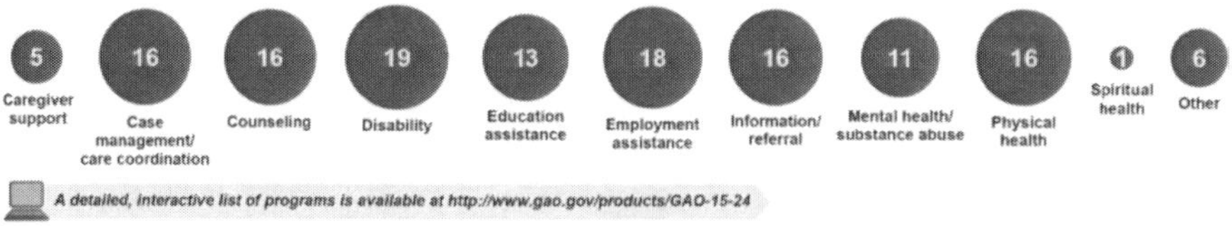

Source GAO analysis of Department of Defence (DOD) and Department of Veterans Affairs (VA) programs. | GAO-15-24

Notes: We separately count programs that share a common name, but are independently implemented by each military service branch. In addition, the number of programs shown by type of services does not total to the 87 that we identified because some programs provide more than one type of service. The frequency of a type of service does not necessarily indicate its utilization.

A detailed, interactive list of programs is available at http://www.gao.gov/ products/GAO-15-24.

Figure 2. Transitioning and Readjusting to Civilian Life: Number of DOD and VA Programs by Type of Services Provided.

We also present the number of programs by type of service provided by each agency in table 3.

Table 3. Transitioning and Readjusting to Civilian Life: Number of Programs Offering Each Type of Service by Agency

DOD	Type of service	VA
1	Caregiver support	**4**
10	Case management/care coordination	**8**
11	Counseling	**7**
5	Disability	**17**
6	Education assistance	**10**
10	Employment assistance	**9**
13	Information and referral	**6**
7	Mental health and substance abuse	**6**
5	Physical health	**12**
1	Spiritual health	**0**
1	Other	**5**

Source: GAO analysis of Department of Defense (DOD) and Department of Veterans Affairs (VA) programs. | GAO-15-24

A detailed, interactive list of programs is available at http://www.gao.gov /products/GAO-15-24.

Notes: The number of programs does not total the 87 we identified because some programs provide more than one type of service. Moreover, the total number of services presented in table 3 does not match the totals in figure 2 because nine programs are jointly administered by the agencies, and we count these programs under each agency. In addition, under type of service, the "Other" category includes services such as housing. For example, the Specially Adapted Housing Grants provide financial assistance to servicemembers and veterans for constructing or modifying a home to meet their adaptive needs. The frequency of a type of service does not necessarily indicate its utilization. See appendix III for the names of these programs.

Nine of the programs are jointly administered by DOD and VA, such as the Pre-Discharge Program for active duty servicemembers or activated National Guard or Reserve members. This program affords these servicemembers the opportunity to file claims for disability compensation up to 180 days prior to separation or retirement from active duty.

Many of the 87 programs we identified not only support servicemembers and veterans but also their families. Of the 87 programs, 35 offer services to the families of servicemembers and veterans, and 5 provide support to the caregivers of wounded, injured, or disabled veterans. These caregivers generally include family members and friends, according to a RAND study.[24]

We Identified 12 DOD and VA Programs That Raise Awareness and Understanding of Servicemembers' and Veterans' Experiences

Using our definition of "program," we identified 12 programs administered by DOD, the military services, and VA that raise awareness and understanding of servicemembers' and veterans' experiences in combat and coming home.[25] DOD and the military services administer 9 of 12 programs, which are listed in table 4.[26] A detailed, interactive list of programs is also available at http://www.gao.gov/products/GAO-15-24.

Table 4. DOD and VA Programs for Raising Civilian Public Awareness of Servicemembers' Combat and Veterans' Readjustment Experiences

Program	Program Description	Agency
Are You Listening?	Helps service providers on Marine Corps installations, such as the staff of installation recreational facilities (e.g., bowling center, fitness center), understand their role in supporting servicemembers; learn methods of effective communication; obtain an awareness of distress and warning signs; and learn about the resources available to assist servicemembers.	DOD – Marine Corps
Army National Guard Funeral and Honors	Renders professional military funeral honors to all eligible veterans when requested by an authorized family member. One of the program's aims is to forge positive relationships between the Army National Guard, state leadership, and local communities.	DOD - Army National Guard
Boss Lifts	Transports employers via military vehicle, aircraft or vessel, to military facilities where they observe National Guard and Reserve members on duty as part of employer outreach efforts.	DOD - Employer Support of the Guard and Reserve (ESGR)

Program	Program Description	Agency
Briefings with the Boss	Brings together employers, unit commanders, ESGR volunteers and community leaders to discuss issues related to service in the National Guard and Reserve.	DOD - ESGR
Heroes Program	Provides community outreach by sharing the courage of servicemembers with the public, as well as recognizing noteworthy acts of bravery performed by them. The program coordinates with radio and web networks across the country to broadcast pre-recorded and live interviews of these military heroes and the situations in which they distinguished themselves.	DOD
Operation: Military Kids (OMK)	Connects military children and youth with local resources to help achieve a sense of community support and enhance their well-being. OMK objectives are to raise community awareness and understanding about how deployment affects military children and to provide education and training to community organizations to better support military children.	DOD - Army
Partnership for Youth Success (PaYS)	Intended to attract quality men and women to serve in an all-volunteer Army, positively impact local perceptions, build an environment more favorable to the Army's brand and to reconnect America with its Army through Army partnerships with America's business community and public sector employers. PaYS partners benefit through access to potential employees who bring the skills, professional work habits, and pride and personal integrity that an Army background provides.	DOD -Army
Post-Deployment Integrated Care Initiative	Provides education and training on post-deployment care and support for returning combat veterans and their families through presentations and trainings for professional organizations, as well as publications and other educational material available to veterans, families, professionals, and the public at large.	VA – Veterans Health Administration (VHA)
Spouse Ambassador Network	Intended to broaden knowledge about military spouse education and career resources in communities where military spouses live and work through collaborations with community organizations. These efforts include creating awareness about the challenges related to military spouse employment.	DOD – Military Community& Family Policy

Table 4. Continued

Program	Program Description	Agency
Statement of Support Program	Aims to help increase employer support by encouraging employers to act as advocates for employee participation in the military through the National Guard and Reserve.	DOD - ESGR
VA Voluntary Service	Programs include: Corporate volunteerism, National Salute to Veteran Patients, Volunteer Transportation Network, and Welcome Home events, among others.	VA
Veterans Justice Outreach	Works to avoid the unnecessary criminalization of mental illness and extended incarceration among veterans by ensuring that eligible justice-involved veterans have timely access to VA services as clinically indicated. Veterans Justice Outreach Specialists are responsible for direct outreach, assessment, and case management for justice-involved veterans in local courts and jails, and liaison with local justice system partners.	VA

Source: GAO analysis of Department of Defense (DOD) and Department of Veterans Affairs (VA) programs. | GAO-15-24

Variation in Definitions Limits the Ability to Compare Our Lists with DOD and VA Inventories

The lists of programs that we developed are generally not comparable with DOD's and VA's 2013 GPRAMA program inventories.[27] As we reported in October 2014, incomparability is due, in large measure, to differences in how agencies defined their programs.[28] OMB's guidance for developing the inventories allowed agencies to define their programs using different approaches, but within a broad definition of what constitutes a "program."[29] The guidance presents possible approaches—by outcomes, customers, products/services, organizational structure, or budget structure—and notes that agencies could use a mix of these approaches. The guidance also notes that agencies and their stakeholders use the term "program" in different ways, and that because agencies have varying missions and achieve their missions through different programmatic approaches, such differences are legitimate and meaningful.

However, as we concluded in October 2014, the flexibility afforded to agencies limits the usefulness of the resulting inventories as a tool for addressing crosscutting issues because the various approaches agencies used to define their programs prevent meaningful comparisons and connections both within and across agencies.[30] As a result, we recommended that OMB take several actions to improve the inventories, such as revising its program inventory guidance to direct federal agencies to collaborate in defining and identifying programs that contribute to common outcomes. OMB staff agreed with this recommendation and said that they will consider how to address it as they move forward with implementation of the program inventory. Once addressed, this recommendation could help facilitate the creation of a more coherent picture of all federal programs that could be used for promoting collaboration and for identifying potential fragmentation, overlap, or duplication, or gaps in services among federal programs or activities.

Within this report, we defined "programs" at a more detailed level than the definition used by DOD and VA for their GPRAMA inventories; that is, we aggregate fewer activities into a program than what is used in DOD's and VA's inventories. DOD and VA described their approaches to define a program as follows:

- DOD uses its budget structures and areas related to each strategic goal, such as Land Forces and Strategic Defense. DOD's program inventory is grouped and aligned to the five DOD strategic goals. The programs are aligned to the strategic goals that they support.
- VA designed its approach to closely mirror the budget structure, which aligns to the way VA manages. The list of programs in the inventory is intended to be recognizable to key external stakeholders, including but not limited to Congress and veterans service organizations.

None of the programs that we identified on our three lists matches any of the 91 programs that DOD identified on its GPRAMA inventory. DOD's inventory is organized by its budget and the strategic goals contained in its 2010 strategic plan.[31] For instance, one goal is "preserving and enhancing the all-volunteer force," and as part of this goal, the strategic plan states that "wounded warrior care" is one of DOD's highest priorities. Under this goal, DOD cites "hospitals and other medical activities"— including "medical care for active-duty personnel in regional defense and non-defense facilities"—as programs. However, DOD's list does not contain any of the programs that we included on our lists, such as the Army Wounded Warrior Program, the Federal Recovery Coordination Program, or Warrior Transition Units.[32] With regard to programs that may raise public awareness and understanding, DOD's inventory cites, "the American Forces Information Service, other personnel support activities dedicated to enhancing morale and improving community relations— including bands and choruses and ceremonial and public relations activities."[33] In contrast, our list includes, for example, the Statement of Support Program and Army National Guard Funeral and Honors program, as noted previously in table 4.

Twenty of 49 VA (or joint DOD-VA) programs we identified that help veterans readjust to civilian life are also listed in VA's GPRAMA inventory. VA's inventory contains 93 programs. Some of the programs on both lists include the Readjustment Counseling at Vet Centers, the Post-9/11 GI Bill, and Vocational Rehabilitation and Employment programs. However, VA's inventory does not include other programs on our lists, such as the Operation Enduring Freedom, Operation Iraqi Freedom, and Operation New Dawn (OEF/OIF/OND) Care Management program and the Transition Assistance Program (a joint DOD-VA program).[34] Only one of the programs on our list of VA programs that raise public awareness and understanding of veterans' readjustment experiences is listed in VA's GPRAMA inventory. As noted above, such differences may be due to differing contexts in which the respective lists were compiled. Such differences in how federal agencies define programs go beyond DOD and VA, as we recently reported in our review of government-wide efforts to implement the federal program inventory.

AGENCY COMMENTS AND OUR EVALUATION

We are not making recommendations in this report. We provided a draft of this product to the Departments of Defense (DOD) and Veterans Affairs (VA) for comment. DOD and VA provided written comments. DOD and VA also provided technical comments that were incorporated, as appropriate.

DOD and VA officials suggested that we include some additional programs. We reviewed these programs and revised the report to include nine additional programs. The following provides more details.

In its comments submitted on October 29, 2014, DOD neither agreed nor disagreed with our findings. In DOD's technical comments, DOD officials suggested that we delete the Directorate of Mental Health under the first objective. We revised the report by removing this program because it is an office, not a program. DOD officials also suggested that we consider including nearly a dozen additional programs under the first or second objectives. After reviewing these programs, we decided not to include several of them because they did not meet the program definitions we had developed for the objectives. However, we revised the report to include six programs under the first or second objectives:

- Under the first objective, we revised the report to include (1) the Comprehensive Soldier Family Fitness (CSF2) program, (2) pre-deployment health assessment, (3) post-deployment health assessment, and the (4) post-deployment health reassessment.
- Under the second objective, we revised the report to include (5) the Army Retirement Services Program and (6) the Army Soldier for Life Program.

In its comments, VA generally concurred with our findings. VA officials suggested additional programs for inclusion under the second objective and provided additional information and examples of its efforts related to employment and raising awareness of benefits available to children and spouses of veterans. Several of these efforts do not focus primarily on helping active duty servicemembers transition or veterans readjust to civilian life. However, we revised the report to include (1) the Automobile and Adaptive Equipment program, (2) Veterans Employment Center, and (3) the VA Liaison for Healthcare Program.

We subsequently reviewed whether any of the nine additional programs that we added to our report were included in the DOD or VA inventories. Only one of the nine programs was included. Specifically, the Automobile and Adaptive Equipment program was included in VA's GPRAMA inventory.

Andrew Sherrill
Director,
Education, Workforce and Income Security Issues

APPENDIX I: SCOPE AND METHODOLOGY

This appendix summarizes our work to identify Department of Defense (DOD) and Department of Veterans Affairs (VA) programs as well as to compare the lists of programs that we generated under objectives 1-3 with DOD and VA's 2013 program inventories that were included in the Office of

Management and Budget's (OMB) program inventory compiled in response to a requirement in the GPRA Modernization Act of 2010 (GPRAMA).

Identifying DOD and VA Programs

To address the first three objectives, we identified DOD and VA programs through the following four-step process:

1. We established a definition for "programs" to clarify the types of DOD and VA programs and activities to be included on our lists because no standard definition of "program" exists. Past GAO work and OMB have defined "program" in very broad terms.[35] For this report, our definitions reflect the specific area of interest specified in the mandate; therefore, we did not attempt to develop a definitive definition.[36] We established a definition for program by reviewing our prior work and other relevant studies on related programs for servicemembers and veterans who have served in recent conflicts.[37] We also obtained input from internal GAO experts on research methods and federal programs for servicemembers and veterans, as well as officials from DOD and VA. In general, we defined "programs or activities" as a federally funded, organized set of activities directed toward a specific purpose or goal that an agency undertakes and is being administered in fiscal year 2014.[38] We further scoped our definition for each of our objectives as follows:
   - Objective 1: DOD or military services' programs or activities that address the effects of combat—including physical, mental, or social heath—on post-9/11 active-duty servicemembers or their spouses or dependents.
   - Objective 2: DOD, military services, or VA programs that focus primarily on helping active duty servicemembers transition or veterans readjust to civilian life.
   - Objective 3: DOD, military services, or VA programs that focus primarily on raising civilian public awareness of the combat experiences of servicemembers and the readjustment experiences of veterans.

For the first objective, we scoped our definition of programs differently than for the second and third objectives. Specifically, for the first objective, although servicemembers and their spouses or dependents must benefit from a program or activity that addresses the effects of combat as we have defined that term, a program or activity does not have to only benefit servicemembers that directly experience combat. For example, the Joint Family Support Assistance Program supports military families who are geographically dispersed from a military installation. This program could support military families in which one or more servicemembers are serving in a combat zone or deployed to Germany (or other noncombat zone) while the family is living stateside. For the second and third objectives, we defined programs as focusing primarily on servicemember transition and veteran readjustment to civilian life as well as efforts to raise public awareness and understanding of servicemembers' and veterans' experiences in combat, coming home, and transitioning to civilian life. An example of such a program includes VA outreach and readjustment counseling services through Vet Centers. VA administers other programs that provide interventions or treatments to help certain veterans, such as the homeless and those contemplating suicide. However, we did not include those types of programs or activities because helping veterans readjust to civilian life is not their primary focus.

For all three objectives we excluded the following types of programs:

- Programs conducting research.
- Programs in which post-9/11 Iraq and Afghanistan servicemembers or veterans are not eligible, such as efforts aimed only at veterans of conflicts or wars prior to Operation Enduring Freedom/Operation Iraqi Freedom/Operation New Dawn (OEF/OIF/OND).
- Programs developed and administered by individual military installations or VA hospitals specifically for the populations they serve at those locations. For example, for the second objective we excluded the Road to Reintegration, a program designed to serve Michigan veterans with a network of resource providers as they return to civilian life. Thus, our findings are limited to the national perspective.
- Programs providing a one-way, passive transmission of information (for example, a directory that lists services available).
- Programs that may have been created or revised to meet our inclusion criteria after fiscal year 2014.

The following further elaborates on these definitions.

General Definition of Terms for Objectives 1–3

- **DOD or military services:** DOD, Office of the Secretary of Defense (OSD) and all subordinate agencies, offices, and programs under DOD; departments of the Army; Air Force, and Navy (including the Marine Corps); the reserve components for each of the military services, including the National Guard. (We exclude U.S. Coast Guard programs because they are administered by the Department of Homeland Security.)
- **VA:** All VA administrations, centers, offices, and programs.
- **Program or activities:** Federally funded, organized set of activities directed toward a specific purpose or goal that an agency undertakes and are being administered in fiscal year 2014. These activities may include assistance for health, housing, employment, and family support, as well as various program types (e.g., direct federal programs, direct federal benefits programs, and grants). In addition, our definition included tax expenditures (credits, deductions, deferrals, or preferential tax rates) that are managed or administered by DOD or VA (and related offices and departments as defined above); however, we did not identify any such programs.
- **Active-duty servicemembers:** Those who are currently serving on active duty in the United States armed forces. This includes activated members of the National Guard and Reserve under Title 10 (full-time duty in the armed forces) or Title 32 (duty performed for which National Guard receives pay from federal government).
- **Veterans:** A person who served in the active military, naval, or air service and who was discharged or released under conditions other than dishonorable. This also includes Title 10 or Title 32 active Guard and Reserve components that have deployed but are still serving in the Reserve Component.
- **Public:** The broader civilian community in the United States, including citizens, public and private employers, police, and court systems.

Specific Definition of Terms for Objective 1

I. Definition: DOD or military services' programs or activities that address the effects of combat—including physical, mental, or social heath—on post-9/11 active-duty servicemembers or their spouses or dependents.

Specific definitions for this objective:

IA. Effects of combat - One or more of the following that results from combat, warfare, or armed conflict:

1. *Physical health* - care for extremity, hearing, vision, burns, or other physical injuries and pain, as well as clinical case management and coordination support.
2. *Mental / emotional health* - care for psychological and brain injuries— such as posttraumatic stress disorder (PTSD) psychotherapies and traumatic brain injury (TBI) treatments—substance abuse, suicide prevention, as well as clinical case management and coordination support.
3. *Social domains* - support for family and caregivers, legal support, non- medical case management, support for reserve components, post-deployment reintegration support for servicemembers and their families, and spiritual support, and other related effects.
4. While servicemembers and their spouses or dependents must benefit from a program or activity that addresses the effects of combat, a program or activity does not have to only benefit servicemembers that directly experience combat. For example, the Joint Family Support Assistance Program supports military families who are geographically dispersed from a military installation. This program could support military families in which one or more servicemembers are serving in a combat zone or deployed to Germany (or other noncombat zone) while the family is living stateside.

IB. Criteria for excluding programs

1. Exclude programs that exclusively provide services to post-9/11 active-duty servicemembers who are transitioning to VA or civilian employment or civilian life (these programs are included in objective 2).

Specific Definition of Terms for Objective 2

II. Definition: DOD, military services, or VA programs or activities whose primary focus is to help post-9/11 servicemembers transition or veterans or deactivated members of the reserve components readjust to civilian life, including their spouses or dependents.

Specific definitions for this objective:

IIA. Primary focus: Key reasons for which the program or activity was designed or created (or one of its main missions or objectives) as stated in the agency's description of the program or activity.

IIB. Help: Assist transition or readjustment through services and efforts, such as:

- providing physical and mental health services;
- counseling and outreach;
- training, job placement and support, employment benefits, and career guidance,
- education benefits;
- campaigns designed to raise awareness of DOD or VA resources available to post-9/11 servicemembers or veterans or their spouses or dependents;
- providing technology like assistive technology, equipment;
- case management, legal support;
- housing benefits/support; and,
- support for family or caregivers, benefits counseling, or other related efforts.

IIC. Civilian Life: Time after separating from the military, including VA care, services, or benefits; nonmilitary employment; or higher education.

IID. Criteria for excluding programs

1. Exclude programs that provide services to post-9/11 servicemembers who remain in the military or transition back to active-duty. (These types of programs are covered in objective 1.)
2. Exclude programs to enhance overall coordination between DOD and VA (e.g., Joint Executive Council).

Specific Definition of Terms for Objective 3

III. Definition: DOD, military services, or VA programs whose primary focus is to raise civilian public awareness of the combat experiences of post-9/11 active-duty servicemembers and the readjustment experiences of veterans.

Specific definitions for this objective

IIIA. Primary focus: Key reasons for which the program or activity was designed or created (or one of its main missions or objectives) as stated in the agency's description of the program or activity.

IIIB. Raise public awareness and understanding

1. Welcome home and reintegration events in communities and college campuses as well as parades and appreciation events aimed at informing the nonservicemember population.
2. Awareness and appreciation campaigns and events as well as public service announcements aimed at civilians, and efforts to educate business leaders about the skills veterans can provide employers, and other related efforts.

IIIC. Criteria for excluding programs

    1. Excludes programs and public awareness campaigns aimed specifically at providing assistance, service, or awareness to servicemembers, veterans or their families. (These types of programs are covered in objective 2.)
    2. Excludes DOD and VA efforts to provide stakeholder assistance to nonfederal entities, such as nonprofits, that provide support or assistance to servicemembers, veterans, and their families.

2. We identified publicly available sources that contain lists of relevant federal programs. We identified these sources based on discussions with DOD and VA officials and internal GAO experts on research methods and federal programs for servicemembers and veterans, as well as through online searches. Table 5 provides the name and description of each source we used by objective.

Table 5. Sources Used to Identify Programs for Objectives 1-3

Source	Description	GAO objective
Caregiver Resource Directory	The 2014 directory provides information in a manner that is intended to enable caregivers to quickly identify many of the available government and nonprofit resources that address their particular needs and requirements.	Objectives 1 and 2
Department of Defense Recovering Warrior Task Force 2012-2013 Annual Report	The Recovering Warrior Task Force (RWTF) issues annual reports on its assessment of the programs and services available to wounded, ill, and injured servicemembers and their family members, from case management through transition to VA and civilian life. The report contains a reference handbook that is intended to provide a baseline familiarity across a wide array of initiatives undertaken on behalf of wounded, ill, and injured servicemembers.	Objectives 1 and 2
RAND, Hidden Heroes: America's Military Caregivers	The RAND report describes the magnitude of military caregiving in the United States, as well as identifies gaps in the array of programs, policies, and initiatives designed to support military caregivers.	Objectives 1 and 2
RAND, Programs Addressing Psychological Health and Traumatic Brain Injury Among U.S. Military Servicemembers and Their Families	The RAND study provides a "snapshot" of all programs sponsored or funded by DOD that address psychological health and traumatic brain injury. The report characterizes these programs; identifies barriers to implementing them fully and maximizing their effectiveness; and provides recommendations for clarifying the role of programs, examining gaps in routine service delivery that could be filled by programs, and reducing barriers that programs face.	Objectives 1 and 2
VA's Federal Benefits for Veterans, Dependents, and Survivors (2013 edition)	The handbook explains disability, pension, health care, education and housing loans, and other benefit programs for veterans and their families, including information on survivors' benefits.	Objectives 1 and 2
DOD and military services' websites	The official websites for DOD and the military services serve as a starting point for finding U.S. military information online.	Objectives 1, 2, and 3
Military OneSource	Military OneSource is a DOD-funded program that provides information and referral to services for military servicemembers and their families through a website as well as counseling. Information includes, but is not limited to, deployment, reunion, relationship, grief, spouse employment and education, parenting and childhood.	Objectives 1, 2, and 3

Source	Description	GAO objective
National Resource Directory (NRD)	The NRD is a partnership among DOD, VA, and the Department of Labor that seeks to connect wounded and other servicemembers, veterans, their families, and caregivers to programs and services that support them. Information contained within the NRD website is from federal, state and local government agencies; veteran and military service organizations; non-profit and community-based organizations; academic institutions and professional associations that provide assistance to wounded warriors and their families.	Objectives 1, 2, and 3
Catalog of Federal Domestic Assistance (CFDA)	The CFDA is a General Services Administration database of federal programs, projects, services, and activities that provide assistance or benefits to the American public. It contains financial and nonfinancial assistance programs administered by all agencies of the federal government. The primary purpose CFDA is to assist users in identifying programs that meet specific objectives of potential applicants and to provide general information on federal programs.	Objectives 2 and 3
VA websites	The official web site for VA serves as a starting point for finding information about VA and its benefits and services online.	Objectives 2 and 3

Source: GAO analysis of publicly available sources identified during the course of our audit work. | GAO-15-24

Note: To identify tax expenditures (credits, deductions, deferrals, or preferential tax rates), we reviewed the list of tax expenditures contained in OMB's Fiscal Year 2015 Analytical Perspectives as well as the Joint Committee on Taxation's Estimates of Federal Tax Expenditures for Fiscal Years 2014-2018. However, we did not identify tax expenditures administered by DOD or VA.

3. We used the definitions and sources from steps 1 and 2 to identify the relevant programs for our lists. For the programs included on our lists, we used the sources identified in step 2 to collect information about the (1) program/activity's name, (2) purpose/objectives, (3) the agency and/or office responsible for its administration, and (4) the population served. For a subset of the programs identified in the searches, we conducted tests to determine the degree to which analysts agreed on the same programs for inclusion. Once we compiled preliminary lists of programs, we provided the lists to internal GAO experts on research methods and federal programs for

servicemembers and veterans for review and comment. We modified the lists accordingly.

Next, a GAO analyst reviewed all of the sources and documented a judgment about whether the programs identified conformed to the definitions we developed in step 1. A second GAO analyst then reviewed separately the assessment and documented an agreement or disagreement with the initial decision. If any differences emerged, the two analysts discussed the differences and made changes based on a verbal resolution of those differences. For any instances in which the two analysts did not resolve differences, a third GAO analyst adjudicated and a final decision was reached.

4. We sent our preliminary list of programs to officials at DOD and VA for comment and verification. Agencies either confirmed that programs on our preliminary lists should be included, identified those that should not be on our lists, or added programs that were not included on our preliminary lists. We modified the lists accordingly.

This four-step process identified 170 separate programs, although some of them are relevant to more than one objective. Specifically, 26 programs are included in more than one objective, such as the Air Force Wounded Warrior Program (AFW2) that addresses the effects of combat and helps wounded and injured servicemembers and veterans transition to civilian life. In addition, some programs share a common name but are independently implemented by each military service branch. For example, the Yellow Ribbon Reintegration Program provides similar services but is independently administered by each service branch. With such programs, we separately counted each military service's program. In carrying out this four step process, we did not conduct an independent legal analysis of the statutory or regulatory basis or requirements for any of the programs we identified. We used the various documentary and data sources to corroborate one another and determined that the documentary and data sources used together were sufficiently reliable for our descriptive purposes.

To help convey our findings, we developed categories to group the types of service provided by the programs. The categories include (1) caregiver support, (2) case management/care coordination, (3) counseling, (4) disability, (5) education assistance, (6) employment assistance, (7) information and referral, (8) mental health and substance abuse, (9) physical health, (10) spiritual health, and (11) other. Because some programs offer more than one type of service, programs can fall into more than one category or service type.

Although a service may be included in many programs or activities, the service may not or may be commonly used by servicemembers or veterans. For example, the Transition Assistance Program (TAP) is one program, but the services provided through the program are widespread because all eligible, transitioning servicemembers are generally required to participate in this program.

Finally, our scope for the first three objectives was limited to identifying DOD and VA programs based on the types of service provided; we did not analyze these programs to identify instances of fragmentation, overlap, duplication, or gaps in benefits or services. In addition, the programs included in our review were accurate and up-to-date when we issued the report. However, some may change over time.

Comparing Lists of Programs

To address the fourth objective, we compared the lists of programs that we generated under objectives 1-3 with DOD and VA's 2013 program inventories—part of OMB's federal program inventory compiled in response to a GPRAMA requirement—to identify similarities and differences between the agencies' inventories and our lists. To help make this comparison, we drew upon prior GAO work on agencies' GPRAMA program inventories. Although this objective was not included in the mandate, we added it because of the parallels between the mandate and the GPRAMA requirement for developing program inventories.

We conducted our work from March 2014 to November 2014 in accordance with generally accepted government auditing standards. Those standards require that we plan and perform the audit to obtain sufficient, appropriate evidence to provide a reasonable basis for our findings and conclusions based on our audit objectives. We believe that the evidence obtained provides a reasonable basis for our findings based on our audit objectives.

APPENDIX II: PROGRAMS ADDRESSING THE EFFECTS OF COMBAT (OBJECTIVE 1)

Program Name	Administering Agency & Unit	Population Served	Type of Service/Assistance											
			Caregiver support	Case management/care coordination	Counseling	Disability	Education assistance	Employment assistance	Information and referral	Mental health and substance abuse	Physical health	Spiritual health	Other	Brief description of "Other"
Air Force Airman & Family Readiness Centers (A&FRC)	DOD/Air Force	Service-member and Family							X					
Air Force Alcohol and Drug Abuse Prevention and Treatment (ADAPT) Program	DOD/Air Force	Service-member								X				
Air Force Chaplain Corps	DOD/Air Force	Service-member and Family										X		
Air Force Reserve Chaplain Program	DOD/Air Force	Service-member and Family										X		
Air Force Suicide Prevention Program	DOD/Air Force	Service-member								X				
Air Force Wounded Warrior Program (AFW2)	DOD/Air Force	Service-member, Veteran and Family		X										

Program Name	Administering Agency & Unit	Population Served	Type of Service/Assistance											
			Caregiver support	Case management/care coordination	Counseling	Disability	Education assistance	Employment assistance	Information and referral	Mental health and substance abuse	Physical health	Spiritual health	Other	Brief description of "Other"
Air National Guard Chaplain Corps (ANG/HC)	DOD/Air Force	Service-member and Family										X		
Air National Guard Psychological Health Program	DOD/Air National Guard	Service-member and Family							X	X				
Army Chaplain Corps	DOD/Army	Service-member and Family										X		
Army Long Term Family Case Management	DOD/Army	Family		X										
Army National Guard Funeral and Honors	DOD/Army and Army National Guard	Family											X	Funeral Honors and benefits
Army National Guard Psychological Health Program	DOD/Army National Guard	Service-member and Family			X					X				
Army Reserve Office of the Command Chaplain	DOD/Army	Service-member and Family										X		

(Continued)

Program Name	Administering Agency & Unit	Population Served	Type of Service/Assistance											
			Caregiver support	Case management/care coordination	Counseling	Disability	Education assistance	Employment assistance	Information and referral	Mental health and substance abuse	Physical health	Spiritual health	Other	Brief description of "Other"
Army Substance Abuse Program (ASAP)	DOD/Army	Service-member and Family							X	X				
Army Suicide Prevention Program	DOD/Army	Service-member and Family							X	X				
Army Wounded Warrior Program (AW2)	DOD/Army	Service-member, Veteran, and Family		X										
Behavioral Health Optimization Project	DOD/Air Force	Service-member, Veteran, and Family							X	X				
Behavioral Health Services in Primary Care	DOD/Army	Service-member			X				X	X				
Child and Youth Behavioral Consultants	DOD/Navy	Family			X					X				
Combat and Operational Stress Control Program	DOD/Army	Service-member and Family								X				

Program Name	Administering Agency & Unit	Population Served	Type of Service/Assistance											
			Caregiver support	Case management/care coordination	Counseling	Disability	Education assistance	Employment assistance	Information and referral	Mental health and substance abuse	Physical health	Spiritual health	Other	Brief description of "Other"
Command Suicide Prevention Program	DOD/Navy	Service-member and Family								X				
Community Care Units (CCUs)	DOD/Army	Service-member		X										
Community Counseling Program (CCP)	DOD/Marine Corps	Service-member and Family			X					X				
Comprehensive Soldier Family Fitness (CSF2)	DOD/Army	Service-member and Family								X				
Comprehensive Combat and Complex Casualty Care Program (C5 Program)	DOD/Navy	Service-member, Veteran, and Family		X						X	X	X		
Computer / Electronic Accommodations Program (CAP)	DOD	Service-member and Veteran				X								
COSC for Families (Conquering Stress with Strength)	DOD/Marine Corps	Service-member and Family								X				
CREDO	DOD/Navy and Marine Corps	Service-member and Family								X		X		

(Continued)

Program Name	Administering Agency & Unit	Population Served	Type of Service/Assistance											
			Caregiver support	Case management/care coordination	Counseling	Disability	Education assistance	Employment assistance	Information and referral	Mental health and substance abuse	Physical health	Spiritual health	Other	Brief description of "Other"
Defense Center of Excellence (DCoE) Outreach Center	DOD/DCoE	Service-member, Veteran, and Family							X	X				
Defense and Veterans Brain Injury Center (DVBIC)	DOD/DCoE	Service-member, Veteran, and Family	X	X					X	X				
Department of Defense and the Armed Services Young Men's Christian Association (ASYMCA) Military Outreach Initiative	DOD/MC&FP	Service-member and Family									X			
Deployment Transition Center (DTC)	DOD/Air Force	Service-member											X	Skills to reintegrate
DES Outreach Attorney Program	DOD/Navy	Service-member				X							X	legal services

Program Name	Administering Agency & Unit	Population Served	Type of Service/Assistance											
			Caregiver support	Case management/care coordination	Counseling	Disability	Education assistance	Employment assistance	Information and referral	Mental health and substance abuse	Physical health	Spiritual health	Other	Brief description of "Other"
DoDEA Student Support Services Branch	DOD/DoDEA	Family			X					X				
DSTRESS Line	DOD/Marine Corps	Service-member, Veteran, and Family							X	X				
DVBIC TBI Recovery Support Program (RSP)	DOD	Service-member, Veteran, and Family	X	X					X	X				
Families Over Coming Under Stress (FOCUS)	DOD/All services	Service-members and Family								X				
Federal Recovery Coordination Program	DOD and VA	Service-member, Veteran, and Family		X										
Fleet and Family Support Center (FFSC)	DOD/Navy	Service-member and Family							X					
Fort Family Outreach and Support	DOD/Army	Service-member and Family							X					

(Continued)

Program Name	Administering Agency & Unit	Population Served	Type of Service/Assistance											
			Caregiver support	Case management/care coordination	Counseling	Disability	Education assistance	Employment assistance	Information and referral	Mental health and substance abuse	Physical health	Spiritual health	Other	Brief description of "Other"
in Transition	DOD/DCoE and VA	Service-member and Veteran							X	X				
Joint Family Support Assistance Program (JFSAP)	DOD	Service-member and Family			X				X					
Marine Awareness and Prevention Integrated Training (MAPIT)	DOD/Marine Corps	Service-member								X				
Marine Corps Combat and Operational Stress Control (COSC) Program	DOD/Marine Corps	Service-member and Family							X	X				
Marine Corps Family Team Building	DOD/Marine Corps	Service-member and Family								X				
Marine Corps Substance Abuse Program	DOD/Marine Corps	Service-member								X				
Marine Corps Suicide Prevention Program	DOD/Marine Corps	Service-member								X				

Program Name	Administering Agency & Unit	Population Served	Type of Service/Assistance											
			Caregiver support	Case management/care coordination	Counseling	Disability	Education assistance	Employment assistance	Information and referral	Mental health and substance abuse	Physical health	Spiritual health	Other	Brief description of "Other"
Marine Corps Wounded Warrior Regiment (WWR)	DOD/Marine Corps	Service-member, Veteran, and Family		X										
Marine Forces Reserve (MARFORRES) Chaplin	DOD/Marine Corps	Service-member and Family										X		
Marine Forces Reserve (MARFORRES) Psychological Health Outreach Program (P-HOP)	DOD/Marine Corps	Service-member and Family							X	X				
Military Adaptive Sports Program (MASP)	DOD/DHA	Service-member				X					X			
Military Families Learning Network: Caregiver Support	DOD/MC&FP	Family	X											
Military and Family Life Counseling Program (MFLC)	DOD	Service-member and Family			X					X				

(Continued)

Program Name	Administering Agency & Unit	Population Served	Type of Service/Assistance											
			Caregiver support	Case management/care coordination	Counseling	Disability	Education assistance	Employment assistance	Information and referral	Mental health and substance abuse	Physical health	Spiritual health	Other	Brief description of "Other"
Military OneSource	DOD/Military Community Outreach	Service-member and Family			X				X					
Military Pathways	DOD	Service-member								X				
Morale, Welfare, and Recreation (MWR) Program	DOD/Military Community & Family Policy	Service-member and Family								X	X			
National Guard Bureau Psychological Health Program	DOD/National Guard	Service-member and Family							X	X				
National Guard Family Program	DOD/Air and Army National Guard	Family							X					
National Guard Office of the Chaplin	DOD/National Guard	Service-member and Family										X		
National Intrepid Center of Excellence (NICoE)	DOD/NICoE	Service-member								X				

Program Name	Administering Agency & Unit	Population Served	Type of Service/Assistance											
			Caregiver support	Case management/care coordination	Counseling	Disability	Education assistance	Employment assistance	Information and referral	Mental health and substance abuse	Physical health	Spiritual health	Other	Brief description of "Other"
Navy & Marine Corps Public Health Center	DOD/Navy and Marine Corps	Service-member							X	X	X			
Navy Chaplin Corps	DOD/Navy and Marine Corps	Service-member and Family										X		
Navy MORE (My Ongoing Recovery Experience) Program	DOD/Navy	Service-member, Veteran, and Family							X	X				
Navy Wounded Warrior Safe Harbor Program	DOD/Navy	Service-member and Family		X										
Office of Airmen's Counsel (OAC)	DOD/Air Force	Service-member				X							X	legal services
Operation: Military Kids (OMK)	DOD/Army	Family							X					
Operational Stress Control Program	DOD/Navy	Service-member and Family							X	X				
Overcoming Adversity and Stress Injury Support	DOD/Navy	Service-member								X				
Pay and Allowance Continuation Program	DOD	Service-member				X							X	Military pay

(Continued)

Program Name	Administering Agency & Unit	Population Served	Type of Service/Assistance											
			Caregiver support	Case management/care coordination	Counseling	Disability	Education assistance	Employment assistance	Information and referral	Mental health and substance abuse	Physical health	Spiritual health	Other	Brief description of "Other"
Pre-deployment health assessment	DOD	Service-member								X	X			
PREP	DOD/Marine Corps	Service-member and Family								X				
Prevention, Treatment and Outreach (PTO)	DOD/Army and Air National Guard	Service-member and Family							X	X				
Post-deployment health assessment	DOD	Service-member								X	X			
Post-deployment health reassessment	DOD	Service-member							X	X	X			
Psychological Health Advocacy Program (PHAP)	DOD/Air Force Reserve and National Guard	Service-member and Family							X	X				
Recovery Coordination Program (RCP)	DOD/All services	Service-member and Family		X										
Respite Care Services	DOD/All services	Family	X											

Program Name	Administering Agency & Unit	Population Served	Type of Service/Assistance											
			Caregiver support	Case management/care coordination	Counseling	Disability	Education assistance	Employment assistance	Information and referral	Mental health and substance abuse	Physical health	Spiritual health	Other	Brief description of "Other"
Returning Warrior Workshop (RWW)	DOD/Navy	Service-member and Family			X				X	X				
Soldier and Family Assistance Centers (SFACs)	DOD/Army	Service-member and Family							X					
Soldiers' MEB Counsel (SMEBC) Program	DOD/Army	Service-member				X							X	legal services
Special Compensation for Assistance with Activities of Daily Living (SCAADL)	DOD/All services	Family	X			X								
Special Psychiatric Rapid Intervention Team (SPRINT)	DOD/Navy	Service-member			X				X	X				
Strong Bonds	DOD/Army	Service-member and Family										X		
Substance Abuse Rehabilitation Program (SARP)	DOD/Navy, Navy Reserves and Marine Corps	Service-member and Veteran			X				X	X				

(Continued)

Program Name	Administering Agency & Unit	Population Served	Type of Service/Assistance											
			Caregiver support	Case management/care coordination	Counseling	Disability	Education assistance	Employment assistance	Information and referral	Mental health and substance abuse	Physical health	Spiritual health	Other	Brief description of "Other"
Survivor Outreach Services	DOD/Army	Family			X									
Traumatic Stress Response (TSR)	DOD	Service-member, Veteran, and Family			X				X	X				
U.S. Navy Reserve Psychological Health Outreach Program (USNR PHOP)	DOD/Navy	Service-member and Family							X	X				
United States Special Operations Command (USSOCOM) Care Coalition	DOD/USSOCOM	Service-member and Family		X										
Vets4-Warriors	DOD/Defense Suicide Prevention Office	Service-member, Veteran, and Family								X				

Program Name	Administering Agency & Unit	Population Served	Type of Service/Assistance											
			Caregiver support	Case management/care coordination	Counseling	Disability	Education assistance	Employment assistance	Information and referral	Mental health and substance abuse	Physical health	Spiritual health	Other	Brief description of "Other"
Warrior Adventure Quest	DOD/Army	Service-member											X	Recreation-al
Warrior Care and Transition Program (WTCP)	DOD/Army	Service-member and Family		X										
Warrior Transition Units (WTUs)	DOD/Army	Service-member and Family		X										
Wounded Soldier and Family Hotline	DOD/Army	Service-member and Family							X					
Wounded Warrior Clothing Support Program	DOD/Army	Service-member				X								
Wounded Warrior Regiment Medical Cell	DOD/Marine Corps	Service-member, Veteran, and Family		X										
Yellow Ribbon Reintegration Program (Air Force)	DOD/Air Force Reserve and National Guard	Service-member and Family							X					

(Continued)

Program Name	Administering Agency & Unit	Population Served	Type of Service/Assistance											
			Caregiver support	Case management/care coordination	Counseling	Disability	Education assistance	Employment assistance	Information and referral	Mental health and substance abuse	Physical health	Spiritual health	Other	Brief description of "Other"
Yellow Ribbon Reintegration Program (Army)	DOD/Army Reserve and National Guard	Service-member and Family							X					
Yellow Ribbon Reintegration Program (Marine Corps)	DOD/Marine Corps	Service-member and Family							X					
Yellow Ribbon Reintegration Program (Navy)	DOD/Navy Reserve	Service-member and Family							X					

Source: GAO analysis of publicly available sources and agency information as confirmed by DOD and VA | GAO-15-24

APPENDIX III: PROGRAMS FOR TRANSITIONING AND READJUSTING TO CIVILIAN LIFE (OBJECTIVE 2)

Program Name	Administering Agency & Unit	Population Served	Type of Service/Assistance											
			Caregiver support	Case management/ care coordination	Counseling	Disability	Education assistance	Employment assistance	Information and referral	Mental health and substance abuse	Physical health	Spiritual health	Other	Brief description of "Other"
Programs Administered by DOD														
Air Force Alcohol and Drug Abuse Prevention and Treatment (ADAPT) Program	DOD/Air Force	Service- member								X				
Air Force Wounded Warrior Program (AFW2)	DOD/Air Force	Service- member, Veteran and Family		X										
Always a Soldier Program (AAS)	DOD/ Army	Service- member and Veteran						X						
Are You Listening	DOD/ Marine Corps	Caregiver	X											
Army Career & Alumni Program (ACAP)	DOD/ Army	Service- member and Family			X			X						

(Continued)

Program Name	Administering Agency & Unit	Population Served	Type of Service/Assistance											
			Caregiver support	Case management/ care coordination	Counseling	Disability	Education assistance	Employment assistance	Information and referral	Mental health and substance abuse	Physical health	Spiritual health	Other	Brief description of "Other"
Army National Guard Psychological Health Program	DOD/Army National Guard	Service- member and Family			X					X				
Army Retirement Services Program	DOD/Army	Service-member and Family			X								X	Retire-ment
Army Soldier for Life Program	DOD/Army	Service-member, Veteran and Family							X					
Army Wounded Warrior Program (AW2)	DOD/Army	Service- member, Veteran and Family		X										
Comprehensive Combat and Complex Casualty Care Program (C5)	DOD/ Navy	Service- member, Veteran and Family		X						X	X	X		
Computer/ Electronic Accommodations Program (CAP)	DOD	Service- member, Veteran				X								
DOD Operation Warfighter Program (OWF)	DOD/OSD	Service- member						X						
DOD Skill Bridge	DOD/ Services	Service- member					X	X						

Program Name	Administering Agency & Unit	Population Served	Type of Service/Assistance											
			Caregiver support	Case management/ care coordination	Counseling	Disability	Education assistance	Employment assistance	Information and referral	Mental health and substance abuse	Physical health	Spiritual health	Other	Brief description of "Other"
DSTRESS Line	DOD/ Marine Corps	Service- member, Veteran and Family							X	X				
Education and Employment Initiative (E2I)	DOD/OSD	Service- member					X	X						
Hiring Heroes Program	DOD/DCPAS	Service- member, Veteran and Family						X						
IRR (Individual Ready Reserve) Marine Outreach Program	DOD/ Marine Corps	Service- member and Veteran			X									
Job Fairs	DOD/ ESGR	Service- member						X						
Marine Corps Wounded Warrior Regiment (WWR)	DOD/ Marine Corps	Service- member, Veteran and Family		X										
Marine for Life	DOD/ Marine Corps	Service- member and Veteran			X									
Medical Care Case Management (MCCM)	DOD/MHS	Service- member		X							X			
Military Adaptive Sports Program (MASP)	DOD/DHA	Service- member				X					X			

(Continued)

Program Name	Administering Agency & Unit	Population Served	Type of Service/Assistance											
			Caregiver support	Case management/ care coordination	Counseling	Disability	Education assistance	Employment assistance	Information and referral	Mental health and substance abuse	Physical health	Spiritual health	Other	Brief description of "Other"
Military OneSource	DOD/Military Community Outreach	Service- member and Family			X				X					
U.S. Navy Reserve Psychological Help Outreach Program (USNR PHOP)	DOD/ Navy	Service- member and Family							X	X				
Navy Returning Warrior Workshop	DOD/ Navy	Service- member and Family			X									
Navy Wounded Warrior Safe Harbor Anchor Program	DOD/Navy	Service-member and Family							X					
Partnership for Youth Success (PaYS)	DOD/ Army	Service- member						X						
Recovery Coordination Program (RCP)	DOD/All Services	Service-member and Family		X										

Program Name	Administering Agency & Unit	Population Served	Type of Service/Assistance											
			Caregiver support	Case management/ care coordination	Counseling	Disability	Education assistance	Employment assistance	Information and referral	Mental health and substance abuse	Physical health	Spiritual health	Other	Brief description of "Other"
Soldier and Family Assistance Centers (SFACs)	DOD/ Army	Service- member and Family							X					
Survivor Outreach Services	DOD/ Army	Family			X									
Troops to Teachers Program	DOD/DANTES and Education	Service- member					X	X						
Turbo Transition Assistance Program	DOD	Service- member			X									
United States Special Operations Command (USSOCOM) Care Coalition	DOD/USSOCO M	Service- member and Family		X										
Warrior Care and Transition Program (WTCP)	DOD/Army	Service-member and Family		X										
Warrior and Family Assistance Center	DOD/ Army Reserve	Service- member and Family		X										
Warrior Transition Units (WTUs)	DOD/Army	Service- member and Family		X										

(Continued)

Program Name	Administering Agency & Unit	Population Served	Type of Service/Assistance											
			Caregiver support	Case management/ care coordination	Counseling	Disability	Education assistance	Employment assistance	Information and referral	Mental health and substance abuse	Physical health	Spiritual health	Other	Brief description of "Other"
Yellow Ribbon Reintegration Program (Air Force)	DOD/Air Force Reserve and Air National Guard	Service- member and Family							X					
Yellow Ribbon Reintegration Program (Army)	DOD/ Army Reserve and Army National Guard	Service- member and Family							X					
Yellow Ribbon Reintegration Program (Marine Corps)	DOD/Marine Corps	Service- member and Family							X					
Yellow Ribbon Reintegration Program (Navy)	DOD/Navy Reserve	Service- member and Family							X					
Programs Administered by VA														
Airborne Hazards and Open Burn Pit Registry	VA/VHA	Service-member and Veteran							X		X			
Allowance for Aid and Attendance for	VA/VBA	Veteran	X			X					X			

Program Name	Administering Agency & Unit	Population Served	Type of Service/Assistance											
			Caregiver support	Case management/ care coordination	Counseling	Disability	Education assistance	Employment assistance	Information and referral	Mental health and substance abuse	Physical health	Spiritual health	Other	Brief description of "Other"
Housebound Veterans														
Automobile and Adaptive Equipment (AAE)	VA/VBA	Service-member and Veteran				X								
Blind Rehabilitation Services (BRS)	VA/VHA	Service-member and Veteran				X								
Building Better Caregivers Workshops	VA/VHA	Caregiver	X											
Clothing Allowance	VA/VHA	Veteran				X								
Coaching into Care	VA/ MIRECC	Caregiver	X											
Compensated Work Therapy	VA/VHA	Veteran		X		X		X						
Comprehensive Assistance for Family Caregivers	VA/VHA	Veteran and Caregiver	X							X	X			
Dependents Educational Assistance Program (DEA) [a.k.a: Survivors' and Dependents' Educational Assistance]	VA/VBA	Family				X	X			X				

(Continued)

Program Name	Administering Agency & Unit	Population Served	Type of Service/Assistance											
			Caregiver support	Case management/ care coordination	Counseling	Disability	Education assistance	Employment assistance	Information and referral	Mental health and substance abuse	Physical health	Spiritual health	Other	Brief description of "Other"
Feds for Vets	VA/VESO	Service- member and Veteran						X						
Grants for the Rural Veterans Coordination Pilot	VA	Veteran and Family								X	X			
Gulf War Registry Health Exam for Veterans	VA/VHA	Service-member and Veteran							X		X			
Home Improvements and Structural Alterations (HISA) Grant	VA/VHA	Veteran				X							X	Housing
Mobile Vet Centers	VA/VHA	Veteran and Family			X					X				
OEF/OIF/-OND Care Management	VA/VHA	Service- member and Veteran		X										
Outreach for OEF/OIF/-New Dawn Veterans	VA/VHA	Service- member			X									
Post 9/11 GI Bill	VA/VBA	Service- member, Veteran and Family					X							

Program Name	Administering Agency & Unit	Population Served	Type of Service/Assistance											
			Caregiver support	Case management/ care coordination	Counseling	Disability	Education assistance	Employment assistance	Information and referral	Mental health and substance abuse	Physical health	Spiritual health	Other	Brief description of "Other"
Post-Deployment Integrated Care Initiative (PDICI)	VA/VHA	Service- member and Veteran		X							X			
Qarmat Ali Medical Surveillance Program	VA/VHA	Veteran							X		X			
Readjustment Counseling (Vet Centers)	VA/VHA	Veteran and Family			X									
Service members' Group Life Insurance Traumatic Injury Protection Program (TSGLI)	VA/VBA	Service-member									X			
SimCoach	VA	Service- member, Veteran and Family								X				
Special Housing Adaptation (SHA) Grants	VA/VBA	Service- member and Veteran				X							X	Housing
Special Monthly Compensation (SMC)	VA/VBA	Veteran and Family				X								
Specially Adapted Housing (SAH) Grants	VA/VBA	Service- member and Veteran				X							X	Housing

(Continued)

Program Name	Administering Agency & Unit	Population Served	Type of Service/Assistance											
			Caregiver support	Case management/ care coordination	Counseling	Disability	Education assistance	Employment assistance	Information and referral	Mental health and substance abuse	Physical health	Spiritual health	Other	Brief description of "Other"
Spinal Cord Injury and Disorders Centers	VA/VHA	Veteran				X					X			
Temporary Residence Adaptation (TRA)	VA/VBA	Service- member and Veteran				X							X	Housing
The Veterans Integration to Academic Leadership (VITAL)	VA	Veteran					X			X	X			
VA Liaison for Healthcare	VA/VHA	Service-member		X							X			
VA for Vets	VA/VESO	Service- member and Veteran						X						
VA Work-study Program	VA/VBA	Service-member and Veteran					X	X						
Veterans Employment Center	VA	Service-member, Veteran, and Family						X						
Veterans Housing - Direct Loans for Certain Disabled Veterans	VA/VBA	Veteran				X							X	Housing

Program Name	Administering Agency & Unit	Population Served	Type of Service/Assistance											
			Caregiver support	Case management/ care coordination	Counseling	Disability	Education assistance	Employment assistance	Information and referral	Mental health and substance abuse	Physical health	Spiritual health	Other	Brief description of "Other"
VetSuccess on Campus	VA/VBA	Veteran		X			X							
Vocational and Educational Counseling for Service members and Veterans	VA/VBA	Service- member and Veteran			X		X	X						
Vocational Assistance	VA	Veteran						X						
Vocational Rehabilitation and Employment (VR&E)	VA/VBA	Service- member and Veteran		X	X	X	X	X						
Programs Administered Jointly by DOD and VA														
All-Volunteer Force Educational Assistance (a.k.a. Montgomery GI Bill (MGIB))	DOD and VA/VBA	Service- member and Veteran					X							
Federal Recovery Coordination Program	DOD and VA	Service- member, Veteran and Family		X										
Integrated Disability Evaluation System (IDES)	DOD and VA/VBA/VHA	Service- member		X		X			X	X	X			

(Continued)

Program Name	Administering Agency & Unit	Population Served	Type of Service/Assistance											
			Caregiver support	Case management/ care coordination	Counseling	Disability	Education assistance	Employment assistance	Information and referral	Mental health and substance abuse	Physical health	Spiritual health	Other	Brief description of "Other"
in Transition	DOD/DCoE and VA	Service- member and Veteran							X	X				
National Guard Bureau Transition Assistance Advisor Program (NGB TAA)	DOD/NGB and VA	Service- member, Veteran and Family			X									
Pre-Discharge Program	DOD and VA/VBA	Service-member				X								
Reserve Educational Assistance Program (REAP)	DOD and VA/VBA	Service-member					X							
Transition Assistance Program (TAP)	DOD, VA/VBA and Labor	Service- member			X		X	X	X					
U.S. Olympic Committee Paralympic Military & Veteran Programs	DOD and VA	Service- member and Veteran				X					X			

Source: GAO analysis of publicly available sources and agency information as confirmed by DOD and VA. | GAO-15-24

End Notes

[1] We use the term "readjustment" to civilian life for purposes of this report: some refer to this instead as "reintegration."

[2] Pub. L. No. 111-352, 124 Stat. 3866 (2011). The acronym "GPRA" in the act's title refers to the Government Performance and Results Act of 1993. Pub. L. No. 103-62, 107 Stat. 285.

[3] We have reported on the implementation of the GPRAMA inventories in a separate body of published work. See GAO, *Government Efficiency and Effectiveness: Inconsistent Definitions and Information Limit the Usefulness of Federal Program Inventories*, GAO-15- 83 (Washington, D.C.: October 31, 2014); and, *Government Efficiency and Effectiveness: Views on the Progress and Plans for Addressing Government-wide Management Challenges*, GAO-14-436T (Washington, D.C.: March 12, 2014).

[4] Pub. L. No. 113-66, § 4, 127 Stat. 672, 689 and National Defense Authorization Act for Fiscal Year 2014 Committee Print, Legislative Text and Joint Explanatory Statement to Accompany H.R. 3304, Pub. L. No. 113-66, pp. III and 579-80.

[5] Although this question was not included in the mandate, we added this objective given the parallels between the mandate and the GPRAMA program inventory requirement.

[6] Included in our list of DOD programs are those administered by the military service branches, which comprise the departments of the Army, Air Force, and Navy (including the Marine Corps); and the reserve components for each of the military services, including the National Guard. We exclude U.S. Coast Guard programs because they are administered by the Department of Homeland Security.

[7] Although the mandate language references "programs," we include "activities" to acknowledge the broad definition of the term "program" and the varying approaches agencies use to achieve their missions.

[8] IDES provides a single set of disability medical examinations designed for determining (1) both fitness and ability to return to duty, and (2) disability for servicemembers who are inhibited from performing their assigned duties as a result of service-connected injury or illness. DOD's assessment of fitness for duty occurs concurrently with the VA disability determination process. Mobile Vet Centers provide individual, group, and family readjustment counseling to combat veterans to assist them in transitioning from military to civilian status through the use of mobile centers, particularly in rural areas.

[9] We scoped our definition of programs and activities for the first objective differently than for the second and third objectives. Specifically, for the first objective, although servicemembers or their spouses or dependents must benefit from a program or activity that addresses the effects of combat as we have defined that term, a program or activity does not have to *only* benefit servicemembers that directly experience combat. For the second and third objectives, we defined programs and activities as focusing *primarily* on servicemember transition and veteran readjustment to civilian life as well as efforts to raise public awareness and understanding of servicemembers' and veterans' experiences in combat, coming home, and transitioning to civilian life.

[10] For all three objectives we excluded (1) research programs/activities; (2) programs or activities for which post-9/11 Iraq and Afghanistan servicemembers or veterans are not eligible; (3) programs and activities developed and administered by individual military installations or VA hospitals specifically for the populations they serve at those locations – thus our findings are limited to the national perspective; and (4) programs or activities that provide a one-way, passive transmission of information (e.g., a directory that lists services available).

[11] The *National Resource Directory* is a partnership among DOD, VA, and the Department of Labor that seeks to connect wounded and other servicemembers, veterans, their families, and caregivers to programs and services that support them. The CFDA is a General Services Administration database of federal programs, projects, services, and activities that provide assistance or benefits to the American public.

[12] We did not include state and local government programs, or other entities' programs, such as nongovernmental organizations as this was not included within the scope of the mandate.

[13] In addition, some programs share a common name, but are independently implemented by each military service branch, such as the Yellow Ribbon Reintegration Program. With such programs, we separately count each military service's program because each program may have varying features.

[14] See GAO-15-83 and GAO-14-436T.

[15] PTSD is a trauma- and stressor-related disorder that develops in reaction to traumatic events and TBI is a physical injury to the brain, often caused by exposure to one or more explosions, or other blows to the head.

[16] Pew Research Center. 2011. *The Military-Civilian Gap: War and Sacrifice in the Post-9/11 Era*. Washington, DC: Pew Social and Demographic Trends; and, Institute for Veterans and Military Families and Institute for National Security and Counterterrorism, "A National Veterans Strategy: The Economic, Social and Security Imperative." Syracuse, NY: Syracuse University.

[17] DOD and VA recently led the Veterans Employment Initiative Task Force, which oversaw the design and development of the revised TAP. Other agencies participating on the Veterans Employment Initiative Task Force include the Department of Labor, the Department of Education, the Office of Management and Budget, the Office of Personnel Management, and the Small Business Administration. A new TAP governance structure, established in October 2013, steers implementation of TAP and will modify the program, as needed, through 2016. The new governance structure is co-led by DOD in 2014 and co-chaired by VA and the Department of Labor. See GAO, *Transitioning Veterans: Improved Oversight Needed to Enhance Implementation of Transition Assistance Program*, GAO-14-144 (Washington, D.C.: March 5, 2014).

[18] See for example, GAO, *Recovering Servicemembers and Veterans: Sustained Attention and Systematic Oversight Needed to Resolve Persistent Problems Affecting Care and Benefits*, GAO-13-5 (Washington, D.C.: November 16, 2012); and *2012 Annual Report: Opportunities to Reduce Duplication, Overlap and Fragmentation, Achieve Savings, and Enhance Revenue*, GAO-12-342SP (Washington, D.C.: February 28, 2012). For additional information, see our Duplication and Cost Savings key issues page at http://www.gao.gov/duplication/overview. *Veterans Affairs: Better Understanding Needed to Enhance Services to Veterans Readjusting to Civilian Life*, GAO-14-676 (Washington, D.C.: September 10, 2014). For reports by others, see VA, 2013 *Performance and Accountability Report*. Department of Veterans Affairs (December 16, 2013); RAND Center for Military Health Policy Research, *Programs Addressing Psychological Health and Traumatic Brain Injury Among U.S. Military Servicemembers and Their Families*. (Santa Monica, CA: 2011); and Institute of Medicine, *Returning Home from Iraq and Afghanistan: Assessment of Readjustment Needs of Veterans, Service Members, and Their Families* (Washington, D.C.: 2013).

[19] One of the Department of Labor's goals is to "Increase the percentage of participants who receive intensive services provided by Disabled Veterans Outreach Program Specialists, with a focus on improving employment outcomes for veterans." Disabled Veterans' Outreach Program Specialists serve veterans through the Jobs for Veterans State Grant Program. See GAO, *Veterans' Employment and Training: Better Targeting, Coordinating, and Reporting Needed to Enhance Program Effectiveness*, GAO-13-29 (Washington, D.C.: Dec. 13, 2012).

[20] GAO-15-83 and GAO-14-436T; OMB, Preparation, Submission, and Execution of the Budget, Circular No. A-11, (Washington, D.C.: July 2012). OMB updated this guidance in its July 2014 revision to the Circular No. A-11.

[21] One of DOD's agency priority goals is "Transition to Veterans." This goal is intended to help fully equip servicemembers for life after the military and reflects both DOD's care for wounded, ill, or injured servicemembers as well as the overall transition of servicemembers

to civilian life. For its part, VA's agency priority goals are to (1) ensure access to VA benefits and services, (2) eliminate the disability claims backlog, and (3) eliminate veteran homelessness.

[22] OMB, Circular No. A-11, *Performance Plans, Performance Reviews, and Annual Program Performance Reports*. (July 2013).

[23] The number of programs providing a service is not necessarily an indication of the number of servicemembers using the service.

[24] RAND, Hidden Heroes: America's Military Caregivers. (Santa Monica, CA: 2014).

[25] Our definition of programs does not include DOD and VA programs that provide informational services—such as web-based or printed materials—involving a one-way transmittal of information. For example, we did not include a VA program that aims to convey to civilians, through web-based testimonials, that success is possible for servicemembers after leaving the military.

[26] Entities other than DOD and VA also offer related programs. For example, Joining Forces is a White House program that asks Americans to get involved in supporting our military's needs in employment, education, wellness, and raising the public's awareness of these issues. Moreover, Veterans Service Organizations, such as the American Legion's Operation Combat Warriors, holds events that raise awareness about veteran transition issues.

[27] OMB and the agencies plan to update these agencies' inventories are on indefinite hold as OMB re-evaluates next steps for how and when to update them.

[28] See GAO-15-83. We also reported that OMB identified 12 different program types (e.g., block grants, direct federal programs) for agencies to assign their programs; however, the list of program types does not include tax expenditures, which represent a substantial federal commitment. Tax expenditures are reductions in a taxpayer's tax liability that are the result of special exemptions and exclusions from taxation, deductions, credits, deferrals of tax liability, or preferential tax rates. For example, we reported that several benefits and services provided to veterans are not taxed, such as disability compensation, Post-9/11 GI Bill benefits, and pension programs. For more information, see our key issues page on tax expenditures at http://www.gao.gov/key_issues/tax_expenditures.

[29] As a starting point, OMB's guidance cites, in part, the definition of "program" contained in GAO's *Glossary of Terms Used in the Federal Budget Process*: "an organized set of activities directed toward a common purpose or goal that an agency undertakes or proposes to carry out its responsibilities." GAO, *A Glossary of Terms Used in the Federal Budget Process*, GAO-05-734SP (Washington, D.C.: September 2005).

[30] GAO-15-83.

[31] DOD's 2010 Quadrennial Defense Review sets the strategic priorities for the agency, including a number of business and management improvements.

[32] Warrior Transition Units provide clinical and non-clinical case management services to wounded, ill, and injured Army soldiers and their families who are expected to require 6 months or more of rehabilitative care, or those who require complex medical management. Individuals are assigned to warrior transition units while they are preparing for transition back to duty or to civilian status.

[33] We excluded programs like American Forces Information Service because they provide a one-way, passive transmission of information.

[34] VA's OEF/OIF/OND Care Management program provides case management and care coordination to recovering servicemembers and veterans, aimed at helping them access resources within VA and the local community. This program is available at all VA Medical Centers.

[35] GAO, *A Glossary of Terms Used in the Federal Budget Process*, GAO-05-734SP (Washington, D.C.: September 2005); OMB, Circular No. A-11, *Preparation, Submission, and Execution of the Budget* (July 2013).

[36] We do not include programs or activities of other federal agencies that may address servicemembers' transition and veterans' readjustment to civilian life and assistance for their families. For example, agencies such as the Departments of Labor, Health Human Services, Housing and Urban Development, as well as the Small Business Administration, and the Internal Revenue Service administer programs that serve and support veterans, such as employment training, housing, and tax credits and deductions. We also did not identify state and local government programs, or other entities' programs, such as nongovernmental organizations because they were not included within the scope of the mandate.

[37] Our list of DOD programs includes those administered by the military service branches, which comprise the departments of the Army; Air Force, and Navy (including the Marine Corps); and the reserve components for each of the military services, including the National Guard. We exclude U.S. Coast Guard programs and activities because they are administered by the Department of Homeland Security.

[38] Although the mandate language references "programs", we include "activities" to acknowledge the broad definition for the term "program" and the varying approaches agencies use to achieve their missions.

In: Support for Servicemembers and Veterans ISBN: 978-1-63484-950-0
Editor: Gayle Marsh

Chapter 2

EMPLOYMENT FOR VETERANS: TRENDS AND PROGRAMS*

Benjamin Collins, Robert Jay Dilger, Cassandria Dortch, Valerie Bailey Grasso, Sean Lowry and Libby Perl

SUMMARY

Veterans' employment outcomes in the civilian labor market are an issue of ongoing congressional interest. This report offers introductory data on veterans' performance in the civilian labor market as well as a discussion of veteran-targeted federal programs that provide employment-related benefits and services.

According to federal data, the unemployment rate for veterans who served after September 2001 is higher than the unemployment rate for nonveterans. Conversely, the unemployment rate for veterans from prior service periods (a much larger population than post-9/11 veterans) is lower than the nonveteran unemployment rate. The varied demographic factors of each of these populations likely contribute to variations in employment outcomes, though their degree of influence is unclear.

There are a number of federal programs to assist veterans in developing job skills and securing civilian employment. Broadly speaking, these programs can be divided into (1) general veterans' programs, (2) programs that target veterans with service-connected disabilities, and (3)

---

* This is an edited, reformatted and augmented version of a Congressional Research Service publication R42790, prepared for Members and Committees of Congress, dated May 11, 2015.

competitive grant programs that offer supplemental services but may not be available to veterans in all areas.

General veterans' programs begin with transition programs that are provided to exiting members of the Armed Forces. These transition programs cover a variety of topics, including information on identifying occupations that align with military skills and specializations, conducting job searches, applying for employment, and navigating veterans' benefits. One of the most common veterans' benefits is educational funding through the GI Bill. The GI Bill programs typically provide funding for tuition, fees, books, housing, and other educational costs while the veteran is enrolled.

Veterans who are seeking employment without obtaining additional education receive priority of service at local federally funded American Job Center (AJC) locations and may receive assistance from dedicated state personnel. Veterans who wish to pursue employment in the federal government are assisted by several policies that give them preference in the competitive hiring process or, in some cases, allow them to forgo the competitive process and be appointed directly. Veterans who wish to start a small business may receive loans and technical assistance from the Small Business Administration (SBA).

Veterans with service-connected disabilities who have obstacles to employment may be assisted by the Vocational Rehabilitation and Employment (VR&E) program. This program provides assistance in identifying an occupation that is consistent with the veteran's skills and interests and providing services (including educational services) to achieve that outcome. Disabled veterans and other veterans with substantial barriers to employment can receive assistance from the Disabled Veterans Outreach Program (DVOP), which funds personnel positions that provide assistance in local labor markets as part of the AJC network.

In addition to these nationwide programs, the federal government also funds competitive grant programs for state, local, and private entities to provide employment-oriented services to veterans. These include the Homeless Veterans Reintegration Program, which provides employment services in conjunction with other supportive services.

BACKGROUND

Veterans' employment outcomes in the civilian sector are an issue of ongoing congressional interest. A number of programs currently exist to assist veterans in obtaining or training for civilian employment. There is regular congressional debate about expanding or otherwise amending these programs to better serve veterans.

This report discusses veterans' employment trends and programs. The first section presents data on veterans' employment outcomes, recent trends, and issues to consider when interpreting veterans' employment data. The subsequent sections present brief discussions of existing programs that provide employment-related services to veterans. These services are divided into (1) general programs that are broadly available to veterans, (2) programs that target veterans with service-connected disabilities, and (3) competitive grant programs that provide additional employment-related services to veterans but may not be available to all veterans.

Notably, this report does not attempt to provide an exhaustive list of all programs that may assist veterans in the labor market, nor does it attempt to provide comprehensive information on the programs it discusses. Instead, it aims to provide a broad overview of the largest employment-related programs as well as other initiatives that may inform future policy. For detailed information on each program, readers are encouraged to refer to the CRS reports or other sources that are referenced in each section.[1]

EMPLOYMENT TRENDS AMONG VETERANS[2]

Estimates of veterans' employment and unemployment are published by the Bureau of Labor Statistics (BLS).[3] The estimates are derived from the Current Population Survey (CPS), a monthly household survey in which respondents may self-identify as veterans. Veterans' employment outcomes are frequently compared to the employment outcomes of nonveterans to establish veterans' relative performance in the labor market.

This section will divide workers into three groups: (1) Gulf War Era II (GWII) veterans who served at any point after September 2001, (2) veterans from prior service periods, and (3) nonveterans.[4] Since these populations vary in many characteristics other than veteran status, comparisons of employment outcomes between these groups should be conducted with caution.

Recent employment outcomes for veterans and nonveterans are presented in *Table 1*. As the table shows, the unemployment rate for GWII veterans is higher than the unemployment rates of both veterans from other service periods and nonveterans. GWII veterans, however, constitute less than one-quarter of the veteran labor force (about 2.5 million of just about 10.7 million).

Table 1. Employment Outcomes by Veteran Status, 2014 Annual Average

	Population (thousands)	Labor Force (thousands)	Unemployed (thousands)	Unemployment Rate
All Veterans	21,229	10,744	573	5.3%
Gulf War Era II Veterans	3,185	2,535	182	7.2%
Other Veterans	18,044	8,209	391	4.8%
Nonveterans	217,820	143,207	8,618	6.0%

Source: Bureau of Labor Statistics, Employment Situation for Veterans—2014, http://www.bls.gov/news.release/ pdf/vet.pdf.

Notes: Gulf War Era II veterans are those who served any time after September 2001. Nonveterans exclude persons under age 18.

Several factors that are not observable in *Table 1* should also be considered when interpreting the employment data in the table.[5]

- *The GWII veteran labor force is younger than the nonveteran labor force.* About 55% of GWII veterans in the labor force are under the age of 35, compared to about 36% of nonveterans in the labor force. Since younger workers generally have higher unemployment rates than older workers, GWII veterans' relative youth may influence their unemployment rate.[6]
- *Veterans have a different educational distribution than nonveterans.* Among those in the labor force, 1% of GWII veterans and 3% of other veterans have less than a high school education, compared to 8% of nonveterans. Conversely, the proportions of college graduates among the labor forces of GWII veterans (33%) and other veterans (31%) are slightly lower than nonveterans (38%).[7] The effect of this different educational distribution on veterans' employment outcomes is unclear.
- *Disability issues.* Approximately 16% of all veterans and 29% of GWII veterans reported service-connected disabilities.[8] Among veterans of all service periods, there was little difference between veterans with service-connected disabilities and veterans without service-connected disabilities in their respective labor force participation rates (45% v. 50%) and unemployment rates (5.9% for each group). Among GWII veterans, veterans with service-connected disabilities were less likely to participate in the labor force (75% v. 87%), though GWII veterans

with service-connected disabilities had a lower unemployment rate than veterans from the same era who did not report service-connected disabilities (5.9% v. 6.6%).[9] Comparable data on employment outcomes for nonveterans with disabilities were not available.

- *Categorization of post-military transition period.* Recent veterans who have not yet secured post-service employment are categorized as unemployed and entitled to unemployment insurance.[10] The classification of this transition period may influence GWII veterans' unemployment rate.

Figure 1 presents recent historical data on unemployment rates for GWII veterans, other veterans, and nonveterans.[11] Several trends emerge over the six-year reference period:

- The unemployment rate for GWII veterans is typically above that of nonveterans, while the unemployment rate for other veterans is below that of nonveterans. The average unemployment rate for the period in the graph was 9.8% among GWII veterans, 6.9% among veterans from other periods of service, and 8.0% among nonveterans. As noted previously, differences in the characteristics of each population may influence their respective unemployment rates.
- The unemployment rate for GWII veterans is more dynamic than the unemployment rate for other populations. While using a 12-month moving average somewhat controls for large variations in monthly estimates, changes in GWII veterans' unemployment rate is still more dynamic than the changes for other populations. This dynamism is likely due to small sample sizes of GWII veterans in the surveys rather than abrupt changes in this population's unemployment rate.
- The unemployment rate for each group trends similarly over the reference period. While the dynamic nature of the GWII veterans' unemployment rate somewhat masks this trend, each group's unemployment rate followed a generally upward trend early in the period covered by the graph and then declined during the later period. The similarity of these trends underscores the influence of the broader labor market on veterans' employment outcomes.

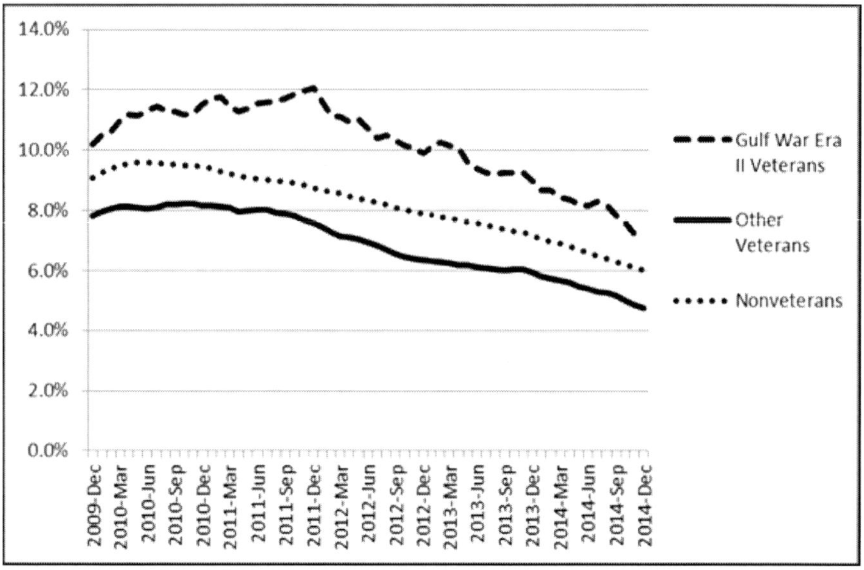

Source: 12-month moving average calculated by CRS based on monthly data from the Bureau of Labor Statistics' Employment Situation historical data for Table A-5, generated at http://www.bls.gov/webapps/legacy/ cpsatab5.htm.

Notes: Data are displayed as the final month of the 12-month moving average. For example, December 2009 is the 12-month period ending in December 2009. Gulf War Era II veterans are those who served any time after September 2001. Nonveterans exclude persons under age 18.

Figure 1. Unemployment Rates by Veteran Status. 12-month moving averages.

EMPLOYMENT-RELATED PROGRAMS FOR VETERANS

This report highlights the primary employment and training services programs that are authorized to improve veterans' employment outcomes. It does not, however, attempt to present a comprehensive list of employment-related programs for veterans. This report emphasizes programs available to veterans of active duty and generally omits discussion of programs that target former members of the military reserve. It also omits discussions of programs or program components that provide benefits to eligible family members of veterans. The final section of this report describes the Work Opportunity Tax Credit, a credit that is currently lapsed but may be reauthorized.

The veteran-targeted programs in this report are presented in *Table 2*. Each is discussed in greater detail in the subsequent text. These programs are grouped into three categories:

- *Programs that are broadly available to veterans.* While they may have some eligibility limitations, these programs are generally available to veterans in all geographic locations, with or without service-connected disabilities;
- *Programs that target veterans with service-connected disabilities.* These programs include the Vocational Rehabilitation and Employment program as well specialized versions of some generally available veterans programs; and
- *Competitive grant programs.* These programs fund employment-related services for veterans but may be limited in scope or geographic availability.

Table 2. Employment-Related Programs, Benefits, and Services for Veterans

Program	Description	FY2015 Funding
General Programs, Benefits, and Services for Veterans		
Transition Assistance Program (TAP) / Transition Goals Plans Success (Transition GPS)	TAP provides services to exiting service members related to obtaining civilian employment and otherwise transitioning to civilian life. The Transition GPS curriculum is currently being implemented within TAP. Transition GPS is mandatory for nearly all exiting service members with expanded services over a five-day curriculum.	$14 million from the Department of Labor (DOL); FY2015 funding levels from the Department of Defense (DOD) and the Department of Veterans Affairs (VA) are not available.[a]
Educational Benefits (GI Bill) Employment Services through the American Job Center (AJC) Network	GI Bill programs generally provide funds for educational costs as well as living expenses while enrolled in educational programs. The most-used program for recent veterans is the Post-9/11 GI Bill. Veterans receive priority of service for all DOL-administered programs, including employment services and	$13.0 billion (estimated)[b] See note[c]

Table 2. (Continued)

Program	Description	FY2015 Funding
	subsidized training through the AJC network. AJC activities are supported by Local Veteran Employment Representatives (LVER) who focus on veterans' issues.	
Priority of Service in DOL training programs	Veterans receive priority of service for any DOL-funded training or employment service program that they are eligible for as members of the general public.	not applicable
Federal Hiring Preferences and Special Hiring Authorities	Veterans receive preference when applying for nearly all competitively-hired federal employment. There are also special hiring authorities in which qualified veterans may be directly appointed to a position that would otherwise be competitively hired.	not applicable
Small Business Administration (SBA) Programs	SBA has a variety of programs to assist veterans with developing and managing a small business, financing a small business, and acquiring federal contracts.	$3.0 million for Veterans' Business Outreach Centers and $7.5 million for the "Boots to Business" training initiative; veterans are also eligible to participate in other SBA training and lending programs
Programs for Veterans with Service-Connected Disabilities		
Vocational Rehabilitation and Employment (VR&E)	VR&E provides funding for training, subsistence, and other expenses to support veterans with service-connected disabilities to pursue an employment outcome or independent living course.	$1.2 billion (estimated)[d]
Disabled Veterans Outreach Program (DVOP)	DVOP funds state personnel positions that provide intensive employment services to disabled and other high-need veterans.	$175 million (also funds LVER)

Program	Description	FY2015 Funding
Specialized versions of other programs	TAP and federal hiring preference have specialized components that target veterans with service-connected disabilities.	Included in general program costs
Competitive Grant Programs that Provide Supplemental Services		
Homeless Veterans Reintegration Program (HVRP)	HVRP provides competitive grants to organizations that provide employment assistance and other	$38.1 million
supportive services to homeless veterans.		
Veterans Upward Bound (VUB)	VUB provides services such as tutoring and application	See note[e]
assistance to aid veterans in preparing for a program of postsecondary education		

Source: Sources are listed in each program's section of this report.

[a] In FY2014, DOD funding was $124 million and VA funding was $103 million.

[b] Program is an entitlement. FY2015 costs are estimated for Post-9/11 GI Bill and Montgomery GI Bill-Active Duty, excluding administrative expenses.

[c] Veterans receive priority of service in DOL-funded employment and training programs, but estimates of the portion of these programs' funds that are used to serve veterans are not available. The Jobs for Veterans State Grant program, which provides funding for DVOP and LVER personnel at AJCs, received an appropriation of $175 million in FY2015.

[d] Program is an entitlement. FY2015 costs are estimates and include benefits and subsistence allowances; they do not include administrative and counseling expenses.

[e] FY2015 funding is not available. FY2014 funding was $13.7 million.

General Veterans' Employment and Training Programs

The programs discussed in this section are available to most veterans of active duty. In the interest of simplicity, this report generally does not present detailed eligibility criteria for each program and benefit, though it does attempt to note eligibility requirements that categorically exclude large numbers of veterans (such as the eligibility window following discharge for GI Bill benefits). This report may omit requirements that would exclude relatively few veterans, such as most programs' exclusion of veterans who were dishonorably discharged.[12] The specific eligibility criteria for each program will usually be available in the external sources that are referenced in the report section that discusses the program.

Transition Programs for Separating Members of the Armed Forces[13]

In 1990, as the post–Cold War drawdown was beginning, Congress authorized a set of benefits and services to assist military personnel in the transition to civilian life.[14] Some of these authorities continued in effect after the drawdown was complete and formed the basis of the Transition Assistance Program (TAP). TAP underwent substantial modification in 2012 and 2013, with the introduction of a revamped curriculum known as Transition GPS.[15] TAP and the new Transition GPS curriculum are both described below.

Transition Assistance Program (TAP)

TAP provides pre-separation services and counseling on a number of transition-related topics to separating members of the Armed Forces.[16] In addition to guidance on broader transition issues such as financial management and health care, TAP includes information on the following employment issues as they relate to veterans:

- the correlation between military skills and civilian occupations;
- professional certifications, including licensing and apprenticeships;
- public and community service opportunities, including federal employment opportunities and veterans' hiring preferences (described in a subsequent section of this report);
- self-employment and entrepreneurship, including veterans' small business and entrepreneurship programs; and
- education and training assistance, including use of veterans' educational benefits and other job training opportunities.

TAP services are provided at many military installations, often found in the military installation's career or family support offices. The Department of Defense (DOD), Department of Labor (DOL), Department of Veterans Affairs (VA), and the Department of Homeland Security (DHS) are each involved in conducting TAP.[17] The curriculum for TAP underwent major revision in 2012. The redesigned curriculum is called Transition GPS, discussed below.

Transition GPS

Transition GPS is the name of the redesigned TAP curriculum brought about by the work of the executive branch's Veterans' Employment Initiative Task Force and intended to conform with the Veterans Opportunity to Work (VOW) to Hire Heroes Act of 2011.[18] Among other changes, the VOW Act made participation in TAP mandatory for nearly all separating military personnel and required that all TAP participants receive "an individualized assessment of the various positions of civilian employment in the private sector for which such member may be qualified" as a result of their military training. These statutory changes took effect on November 21, 2012, one year after the enactment of the VOW Act.

DOD introduced the Transition GPS pilot program at seven military bases in the summer of 2012, and it is now conducted at major military installations across the country and overseas. It includes a five-day core program that incorporates the elements of TAP described above into a redesigned curriculum that is intended to ensure that servicemembers are "career ready" when they leave military service. The core curriculum includes the following modules: pre-separation counseling (4 hours), VA benefits[19] (6 hours), employment workshop (24 hours), financial planning (4 hours), resilient transition (1 hour), and a crosswalk between military and civilian skills that includes a "skills gap" analysis (2 hours). Servicemembers are also required to develop an individual transition plan and participate in a "capstone event." The capstone event verifies that the servicemember meets career readiness standards and has a viable individual transition plan.[20]

Some of the key differences between the "legacy" TAP curriculum and the new Transition GPS curriculum include the following:

- The five-day core curriculum is mandatory, not optional, for nearly all separating servicemembers.
- Class sizes are smaller than under the previous curriculum to provide individual attention.
- The required individual transition plan is standardized and tied to the servicemember's personal goals.
- Successful completion is based on achieving "career readiness standards," not simply attendance.
- The program concludes with a capstone event that verifies that each servicemember meets career readiness standards and has a viable individual transition plan.

- In addition to the core curriculum, servicemembers are able to participate in optional tracks for higher education, entrepreneurship, and technical training, each of which last two days. Servicemembers can participate in all three optional tracks if they so desire.

The "core" Transition GPS curriculum was implemented in November 2012. Implementation of the optional tracks began in 2013.

Credentialing of Servicemembers and Transfer of Military Skills

There are ongoing efforts to align military training and experience with civilian credentials and licenses. These efforts can enable members of the Armed Forces to obtain civilian credentials while enlisted or apply military experience to civilian licensing requirements after discharge.

The armed forces have several initiatives to increase enlisted personnel's access to civilian credentials. Section 548 of P.L. 112-81, the FY2012 National Defense Authorization Act, (as amended by Section 543 of P.L. 112-239, FY2013 NDAA), required the Secretary of Defense:

> [T]o carry out a pilot program to assess the feasibility and advisability of permitting enlisted members of the Armed Forces to obtain civilian credentialing or licensing for skills required for military occupational specialties (MOS) or qualification for duty specialty codes.[21]

DOD selected five civilian occupational areas for inclusion in the pilot program: aircraft mechanics, automotive mechanics, health care support, logistics and supply, and truck driving. These occupational specialties were selected, in part, because of the size of the labor forces in each group, as well as the projected outlook for both medium to high wages and a projected need. The interim and final reports on the Pilot program were issued in 2013.[22]

The Armed Forces are building on the pilot program to develop credentialing opportunities for other military occupational specialties.[23] Credentials aligned with military service can include (1) non-DOD government licenses, such as a commercial drivers' license (CDL) issued by a state government or (2) certification from an independent, industry-recognized agency, such as the American Welding Society. Recently, the Army issued Army Directive 2015-12, which provides guidance on implementing a credentialing program and a Career Skills Program.[24]

There have also been efforts to translate military training and skills to civilian credentials after a member separates from the Armed Forces. Most occupational licenses are issued at the state level. State programs that consider military training and experience in the context of licensing requirements are at various stages of development.[25] In the case of licenses that are issued by the federal government, the Veterans Skills to Jobs Act (P.L. 112-147) specifies that federal licensing authorities shall consider and may accept "any relevant training received by [a veteran] while serving as a member of the armed forces, for the purpose of satisfying the requirements for such license."

GI Bill Educational Assistance Programs[26]

The VA administers several educational assistance programs for veterans (commonly known as GI Bills) that are intended to avert unemployment, adjust veterans to civilian life, reward military service, encourage recruitment and retention in the military, and make education affordable. VA educational assistance payments are available for approved programs of education as well as living expenses while enrolled.[27]

While there are several GI Bill programs, the vast majority of veterans who utilize education benefits do so under the Post-9/11 GI Bill or the Montgomery GI Bill-Active Duty (MGIB-AD). Both programs provide benefits for 36 months of full-time schooling or the equivalent in part-time attendance.[28] The Post-9/11 GI Bill provides separate payments for tuition and fees, supplies, housing, and other costs. The maximum benefit for tuition and fees at a public institution of higher learning is equal to in-state tuition and fees for that program of education. As of August 1, 2014, the maximum benefit for tuition and fees at a private or foreign institution is $20,235 per academic year. The monthly housing allowances under the Post-9/11 GI Bill varies by geographical location and range from about $800 to about $3,700.[29] MGIB-AD provides a single monthly payment to the veteran to cover both education and living expenses. As of October 1, 2014, the maximum benefit under MGIB-AD is $1,717 per month.

Post 9/11 GI Bill benefits are typically available within 15 years of discharge or release from active duty. MGIB-AD benefits (and most other GI Bill benefits) are generally available within 10 years. Notably, GI Bill benefits are not considered when calculating a student's eligibility for need-based Pell Grants, meaning that a veteran who meets Pell Grant criteria may receive both Pell Grants and GI Bill benefits.[30] As an additional benefit, educational assistance received under a VA education program (including subsistence or housing allowances for enrolled veterans) is not subject to federal income tax.

In its FY2016 budget, the VA estimated that total FY2015 benefits for the Post-9/11 GI Bill and MGIB-AD would be $13.0 billion.[31]

Services Through the American Job Center Network

Most federal employment programs are administered through a network of approximately 2,500 local American Job Centers (AJCs, also known as One-Stop Career Centers).[32] Most AJC partner programs are administered at the federal level by the DOL. Federal law requires that veterans receive priority of service in all DOL programs for which they are qualified.[33] In practice, this means that veterans have ready access to most AJC-administered programs, including job search assistance, case management, and subsidized training.[34]

In 2011, DOL further operationalized veterans' priority of service in the AJC system by launching a Gold Card initiative directed at post-9/11 veterans. In addition to priority in all training programs, the initiative also provides veterans with specific intensive employment services such as job readiness assessments, career guidance, and referral to training through federal or state programs. Qualified veterans may also receive six months of follow-up services from a case manager.[35]

Jobs for Veterans State Grants

The Jobs for Veterans State Grants (JVSG) program provides formula grants to states to fund two types of personnel positions that work in conjunction within the AJC system to assist veterans.

1. *Local Veterans Employment Representatives* (LVER) conduct outreach to employers on behalf of veterans and facilitate employment, training, and placement services through the state workforce system. LVER staff may provide referral to other benefits and services (such as the GI Bill) and may assist other AJC personnel in developing strategies to assist veterans.
2. *Disabled Veterans Outreach Program* (DVOP) personnel provide intensive employment services (such as case management) to veterans with barriers to employment. Disabled veterans receive the highest priority in services, though other veteran populations with significant barriers to employment (such as homelessness or a lack of high school diploma or equivalent) may also be served by DVOP personnel.

In FY2015, $175 million was appropriated for JVSG activities.

Online Veterans Employment Center

In April 2014, President Obama announced the launch of a Veterans Employment Center on the VA website.[36] The site provides online tools that can assist veterans in searching for local jobs, building a resume, and identifying civilian jobs that correspond with their military skills and specialties. The site also provides referrals to many of the federal services and benefits described in this report.[37]

Federal Employment[38]

There are several programs and policies that provide a preference for veterans in obtaining employment in the federal government. These policies and programs can either give veterans an advantage in the competitive hiring process or, in some cases, allow a veteran to be appointed without going through the competitive process.

Preference in Competitive Hiring

In the federal hiring process for competitive positions, veterans may receive preference in the assessment of their applications. The specifics of the preference depends on the process through which the application is assessed and the specifics of the veteran applicant's service.

In instances where applications are assessed a numerical score based on the applicant's qualifications, veterans may receive points in addition to their assessed score. A five point-preference is available to veterans who served during a war or in specified campaigns.[39] A 10- point preference is available to veterans who either (1) have a service-connected disability or (2) received a Purple Heart. The 10-point preference is available to these veterans regardless of their period or location of service. Typically, the maximum numerical score of an application is 100 points, though veterans' preference can raise a veteran applicant's score over 100.

In other instances, the application assessment process may forgo the points system and instead evaluate applicants using a *category rating* system in which applicants are assigned to categories based on their qualifications (e.g., not qualified, qualified, or highly qualified). In these instances, veterans' preference is operationalized by listing preference-eligible veterans ahead of all nonpreference-eligible in the same qualification category.[40] In this process, veterans with service-connected disabilities are listed ahead of veterans without service-connected disabilities.

Special Hiring Authorities

There are several hiring programs that allow qualified veterans to be appointed to what would otherwise be competitive federal positions without having to compete with the general public. Typically, these programs allow an agency to hire a veteran in a shorter period of time than it would take to fill the position through the competitive service process. To be eligible for these special hiring authorities, a veteran must have been separated from the Armed Forces for less than three years, have served in a qualified combat mission, or be disabled.[41]

Other Initiatives

In 2009, President Barack Obama issued Executive Order 13518, which aimed to "enhance recruitment of and promote employment opportunities for veterans within the executive branch."[42] The program established a Council on Veterans Employment that included 24 agencies and required each agency to develop an agency-specific plan and designate an office or officer for promoting employment opportunities for veterans within the agency. The order also established a website that offered veteran-specific information on obtaining federal employment as well as contact information for the individual or office in each agency responsible for promoting veterans' employment within the agency.[43]

Small Business Administration Programs[44]

The Small Business Administration (SBA) has a variety of programs to assist veterans with developing and managing a small business, financing a small business, and acquiring federal contracts. Congressional interest in these programs has increased in recent years primarily due to reports by veteran organizations that veterans were experiencing difficulty accessing the SBA's programs, as well as general interest in facilitating the transition of veterans from military to civilian life.

In an effort to assist veteran entrepreneurs, the SBA has either provided or supported management and technical assistance training for veteran-owned small businesses since its formation as an agency.[45] In FY2014, the SBA provided management and technical assistance training services to more than 100,000 veterans through its various management and technical assistance training partners (e.g., Small Business Development Centers, Women's Business Centers, SCORE (Service Corps of Retired Executives), and Veterans Business Outreach Centers (VBOCs)).[46] In addition, the SBA's Office of Veterans Business Development administers several programs to assist veteran-owned businesses, including the Boots to Business program, which is an elective track within the Department of Defense's Transition Goals, Plans, Success (Transition GPS) program.[47]

Also, in an effort to enhance small business owners' access to capital, since October 1, 2013, the SBA has waived the up-front, one-time loan guaranty fee on all SBA 7(a) loans of $150,000 or less (benefitting both veteran and non-veteran small business owners).[48] Since January 1, 2014, the SBA has also waived the upfront, one-time loan guaranty fee for all veteran loans under the SBAExpress program (called the Veterans Advantage Program).[49] The Obama Administration announced that the SBAExpress veteran fee waiver is part "of SBA's broader efforts to make sure that veterans have the tools they need to start and grow a business."[50]

The SBAExpress program is designed to increase the availability of credit to small businesses by permitting lenders to use their existing documentation and procedures in return for receiving a reduced SBA guaranty on loans.[51] It provides a 50% loan guaranty on loan amounts up to $350,000, which is less than the guaranty of up to 85% of loans of $150,000 or less and up to 75% of loans of $150,001 to the statutory limit of $5 million provided by the SBA's main 7(a) loan guaranty program.

Since October 1, 2014, the SBA has also provided veterans a 50% discount of the upfront, onetime loan guaranty fee for all non-SBAExpress 7(a) loans above $150,000. The Obama Administration has indicated that it plans to extend all three of these fee waivers through FY2016.[52]

The SBA also assists veterans through its Military Reservist Economic Injury Disaster Loan Program (MREIDL), which supplements its general, direct-loan disaster lending program. MREIDL provides disaster assistance in the form of direct loans of up to $2 million to help small business owners who are not able to obtain credit elsewhere to meet ordinary and necessary operating expenses that they could have met but are not able to meet because an essential employee has been called up to active duty in his or her role as a military reservist or member of the National Guard due to a period of military conflict.[53]

The SBA also assists small businesses, including service-disabled veteran-owned small businesses, in acquiring federal contracts through its management and oversight of the federal government's procurement goals for small businesses.[54] Under the goaling program, at least 3% of the total value of all small-business-eligible prime contract awards and subcontract awards are supposed to be awarded to small businesses owned and controlled by service-disabled-veteran owned small businesses.[55]

Programs for Veterans with Service-Connected Disabilities

Additional employment services exist for veterans with service-connected disabilities. The Vocational Rehabilitation and Employment (VR&E) program provides comprehensive services for veterans with a service-connected disability and does not have an analogue among general veterans' programs. Other programs for disabled veterans are specialized variations of general programs that were discussed previously.

Vocational Rehabilitation and Employment (VR&E)[56]

VR&E provides job training and employment services to veterans who have service-connected disabilities.[57] To be entitled to VR&E services, a veteran with a service-connected disability must also demonstrate an employment handicap that hinders the veteran's ability to prepare for, obtain, or retain employment consistent with his or her abilities, aptitudes, and interests.

VR&E offers several tracks of services, depending on the veteran's employment objective and needs. Veterans who already have the necessary job skills or seek to return to previous employment can receive short-term services such as resume assistance and job accommodations. Veterans who need job skills are eligible for education and training benefits as well as employment services once they complete training. The VA has reported that long-term services, including education and training, is the most-utilized VR&E track.

In FY2015, mandatory VR&E benefits are estimated to be approximately $1.2 billion. FY2015 discretionary expenditures in support of the VR&E program (primarily counseling and support services) are estimated to be $313 million.[58]

Disabled Veterans Outreach Program (DVOP) Employment Services[59]

DVOP provides formula grants to states to hire staff to provide a range of intensive services to veterans with service-connected disabilities as well as other veterans with multiple barriers to employment.[60] Services include case management, referral to other service providers (e.g., the VA's VR&E program discussed in the prior subsection), employment counseling, and job search assistance.

DVOP is part of DOL's JVSG program, which also funds the previously discussed LVER program.[61] In FY2015, JVSG's budget authority was approximately $175 million. JVSG is funded out of the Employment Security Administration Account in the Unemployment Trust Fund.

Components of General Programs That Target Disabled Veterans

Several of the broader veterans' programs described previously in this report have specialized components for disabled veterans. Additional detail can be found in the sources referenced in each program's primary section of this report.

- *Transition Assistance Program.* TAP and the Transition GPS curriculum provide specialized services for exiting service members with service-connected disabilities.
- *Federal Employment.* As discussed in the section above, veterans with service-connected disabilities are eligible for the highest preference in competitively hired federal positions. Disabled veterans are also eligible for special hiring authorities, including noncompetitive appointments for qualified veterans with a disability rating of 30% or more from the VA.[62]
- *Work Opportunity Tax Credit* (currently lapsed; see WOTC section for full details). Some WOTCs were available for businesses that hired veterans who were eligible for disability compensation from the VA. The largest available tax credits were for hiring a veteran who was eligible for disability compensation and who was unemployed for at least six of the 12 months prior to hire.

Veteran-Targeted Competitive Grant Programs

Additional programs provide competitive grants for entities that provide services to veterans. Since the programs are competitive grants, they may be available only in certain areas, may have limited capacity, or may serve only a targeted veteran population.

Homeless Veterans Reintegration Program (HVRP)[63]

HVRP is a competitive grant program administered by DOL. The HVRP program has two goals: (1) assisting veterans in achieving meaningful employment, and (2) assisting in the development of a service delivery system to address the problems facing homeless veterans.

HVRP grantee organizations provide services that include outreach, assistance in drafting a resume and preparing for interviews, job search assistance, subsidized trial employment, job training, and follow-up assistance after placement. Recipients of HVRP grants also provide supportive services not directly related to employment such as transportation, provision of assistance in finding housing, and referral for mental health treatment or substance abuse counseling.

FY2015 appropriations for HVRP were $38.1 million.

TRIO Veterans Upward Bound (VUB)[64]

The TRIO Veterans Upward Bound (VUB) program provides services to assist veterans in preparing for programs of postsecondary education. VUB projects provide academic instruction, tutoring, assistance in completing secondary school, assistance with college admissions and applications, and assistance applying for financial assistance. It is administered by the Department of Education (ED).

To be eligible for participation, veterans must be in need of academic support to pursue education beyond secondary school successfully. At least two-thirds of program participants must be low-income, potential first-generation college students. The remaining one-third of participants must be either low-income, potential first-generation college students, or otherwise be at risk of academic failure. The program defines a veteran who is at risk for academic failure as an individual who has been out of high school or dropped out of a program of postsecondary education for five or more years, has scored on standardized tests below the level that demonstrates a likelihood of success in a program of postsecondary education, or meets the definition of an individual with a disability.

Final data on the portion of FY2015 TRIO funding that was allocated to VUB projects are not available. In FY2014, ED allocated $13.7 million of the $838 million in TRIO appropriation to VUB projects.[65]

Programs that are Currently Lapsed

Work Opportunity Tax Credit (WOTC) for Employers[66]

The WOTC provided a tax credit for employers who hired qualified veterans. In cases where the eligible hire worked at least 400 hours, the credit was equal to 40% of the wages paid to the eligible veteran, up to a certain level.[67]

Authorization for WOTC expired after December 31, 2014. In the past, WOTC has expired and then been retroactively reauthorized with other tax provisions ("tax extenders").[68]

DOL issued guidance on January 7, 2015, noting that state agencies may continue to accept new WOTC applications, but that they must postpone final processing of the applications.[69] These applications may be processed if Congress enacts the WOTC for 2015.

Under the most recent authorization (which expired after December 31, 2014), the criteria and credit amounts for veterans were:

- a maximum credit of $2,400 for hiring a veteran who was receiving Supplemental Nutrition Assistance Program (SNAP; formerly food stamps) benefits for at least three months during the year prior to hire;
- a maximum credit of $2,400 for hiring a veteran who had been unemployed for a total of at least four weeks but less than six months in the year prior to hire;
- a maximum credit of $4,800 for hiring a veteran who was eligible for disability compensation from the VA and was within one year of discharge or release from military duty;
- a maximum credit of $5,600 for hiring a veteran who had been unemployed for a total of at least six months in the year prior to hire; and
- a maximum credit of $9,600 for hiring a veteran who was eligible for disability compensation from the VA and who had been unemployed for a total of six months in the year prior to hire.

End Notes

[1] References also include a CRS analyst to contact about the topic. In cases where a topic does not list a contact, inquiries should be directed to the coordinator of this report.

[2] This section was prepared by Benjamin Collins, Analyst in Labor Policy, bcollins@crs.loc.gov, 7-7382.

[3] The data discussed in this section are mostly 2014 annual averages. BLS publishes monthly employment estimates for veterans, though these monthly estimates lack the demographic detail of its annual estimates. The most recent monthly estimates of veterans' employment are always available at http://www.bls.gov/web/empsit/cpseea40.htm.

[4] The designation of Gulf War Era II veterans follows the definition set by the Bureau of Labor Statistics. Data for veterans from other periods were calculated by subtracting Gulf War Era II veterans data from total veterans data. Nonveterans data are limited to persons age 18 and over.

[5] Data on veterans' characteristics are from BLS, "Employment Situation of Veterans—2013," March 20, 2014, http://www.bls.gov/news.release/vet.htm.

[6] Ibid., Table 2A. In 2014, the unemployment rates for both GWII veterans under the age of 35 as well as nonveterans under the age 35 were each 8.7%.

[7] Ibid., Table 3. Data only consider veterans age 25 and over. About 11% of the GWII veterans in the labor force are under the age of 25.

[8] Ibid., Table 7. Approximately 19% of veterans did not report their disability status. These data are from a one-month supplement to the CPS with an August 2014 reference period. Since the one-month reference period is different from the one-year reference period of the other data, these data on veterans with service-connected disabilities are not directly comparable to the other employment data in this report.

[9] Ibid. Table 6.

[10] For more information on unemployment insurance for former members of the armed services, see CRS Report RS22440, Unemployment Compensation (Insurance) and Military Service, by Julie M. Whittaker.

[11] The reference period was determined by the earliest availability of monthly data for GWII veterans.

[12] For a more detailed discussion of factors that may influence a former service member's eligibility for veterans' benefits, see CRS Report R42324, Who is a "Veteran"?—Basic Eligibility for Veterans' Benefits, by Umar Moulta-Ali.

[13] Inquiries related to transition programs should be directed to Valerie Bailey Grasso, 7-7614, vgrasso@crs.loc.gov. This section was originally written by Lawrence Kapp.

[14] Codified at 10 U.S.C. 1141-1150.

[15] Department of Veterans Affairs, "Redesigned Transition Assistance Program Announced," July 23, 2012, available at http://www.va.gov/opa/pressrel/pressrelease.cfm?id=2360.

[16] Formerly, TAP also included a program called Disabled Transition Assistance Program (DTAP), which provided individual instruction for disabled servicemembers regarding their job-readiness and special needs they might have as a result of their disability, along with information on the VA's Vocational Rehabilitation and employment services. DTAP was incorporated into the VA benefits segment of the new Transition GPS curriculum in 2012.

[17] Memorandum of Understanding between the Department of Labor, Department of Defense, Department of Veterans Affairs, and Department of Homeland Security, "Transition Assistance Program and Disabled Transition Assistance Program," signed September 19, 2006, available at http://www.dol.gov/vets/vpls/VPL%20Attachments/VPL%201-08%20Attch%201%20-%20Transition%20Assistance%20and%20Disabled%20Transition%20Assistance%20Programs%20Memorandum%20 of%20Understanding%20dated%20September%2019,%202007..pdf.

[18] The VOW to Hire Heroes Act is Title II of P.L. 112-56. In addition to modifying TAP, the law had other provisions related to veterans' employment.

[19] As part of the VA benefits briefing, each participant is required to set up a VA benefits account online.

[20] If servicemembers have not met the career readiness standards or created viable transition plans, the capstone event will ensure they are referred for appropriate training or remedial assistance.

[21] Section 558 of P.L. 112-81, the FY2012 NDAA, enacted into law on December 31, 2011.

[22] U.S. Department of Defense, Pilot Program: Civilian Credentialing for Military Occupational Specialties: A Report in Response to Section 558 of the National Defense Authorization Act for Fiscal Year 2012, P.L. 112-81 (as amended by Section 543 of the FY2013 NDAA, P.L. 112-239), Volumes 1 and 2, September 27, 2013.

[23] Michelle Tan, "Army to Create Certifications or Licenses for every MOS." Army Times, March 24, 2015. Accessed online at http://www.armytimes.com/story/military/careers/army/enlisted/2015/03/23/army-credentialing-every-mos/25049105.

[24] Secretary of the Army, Army Directive 2015-12, Implementation Guidance for Credentialing Program and Career Skills Program, Memorandum for Distribution, March 11, 2015, accessed online at http://www.apd.army.mil/pdffiles/ad2015_12.pdf.

[25] The National Governors Association documents state-level best practices as part of its Veterans' Licensing and Certification Policy Academy.

[26] For more information on each of the GI Bills, see CRS Report R42785, GI Bills Enacted Prior to 2008 and Related Veterans' Educational Assistance Programs: A Primer, by Cassandria Dortch; and CRS Report R42755, The Post-9/11 Veterans Educational Assistance Act of 2008 (Post-9/11 GI Bill): Primer and Issues, by Cassandria Dortch.

[27] Eligible educational programs include but are not limited to college courses, vocational programs, entrepreneurship courses, apprenticeships, on-the-job training, and licensing or certification tests.

[28] Benefits can be used in nonconsecutive months. For example, a veteran may use GI Bill benefits for four traditional nine-month full-time academic years.

[29] Monthly housing allowances under the Post-9/11 GI Bill equal the monthly basic allowance for housing for a member of the Armed Forces with dependents in pay grade E-5 in the military housing area in which the veteran's educational institution is located. Local rates are available at http://www.defensetravel.dod.mil/site/bah.cfm.

[30] For more information on Pell Grants, see CRS Report R42446, Federal Pell Grant Program of the Higher Education Act: How the Program Works and Recent Legislative Changes, by Cassandria Dortch.

[31] The FY2016 VA budget is available at http://www.va.gov/budget/products.asp.

[32] For more information on the AJC network, see http://jobcenter.usa.gov/.

[33] Priority of service means that that a veteran (or the qualified spouse of a veteran) "shall be given priority over nonveterans for the receipt of employment, training, and placement services provided under [a DOL-administered] program, notwithstanding any other provision of law." Priority of service was established by The Jobs for Veterans Act of 2002 (P.L. 107-288) and is codified at 38 U.S.C. 4215.

[34] For a discussion of AJC-administered programs, see CRS Report R43301, Programs Available to Unemployed Workers through the American Job Center Network.

[35] More information on the Gold Card initiative is available at http://www.dol.gov/vets/goldcard.html.

[36] "Obama Administration Launches Online Veterans Employment Center: One-Stop-Shop Connects Veterans, Transitioning Service Members, and their Spouses to Employers," April 23, 2104, at http://www.whitehouse.gov/thepress-office/2014/04/23/obama-administration-launches-online-veterans-employment-center-one-stop.

[37] The website is hosted by the VA at https://www.ebenefits.va.gov/ebenefits/jobs.

[38] For a more in-depth discussion of federal employment for veterans, see archived CRS Report RS22666, Veterans Benefits: Federal Employment Assistance, by Christine Scott.

[39] Applicable dates and criteria are available from the Office of Personnel Management at http://www.opm.gov/staffingportal/vetguide.asp#2When.

[40] For some jobs, a veteran with service-connected disability who is assessed lower qualification category may "float" to the top of the highest qualification category.

[41] Full details on these hiring authorities is available from the Office of Personnel Management at http://www.opm.gov/staffingportal/vetguide.asp#6.

[42] The full text of the order, including a list of participating agencies, is available at http://www.gpo.gov/fdsys/pkg/FR2009-11-13/pdf/E9-27441.pdf.

[43] See http://www.fedshirevets.gov/AgencyDirectory/index.aspx for a list of agency contacts.

[44] This section was prepared by Robert Jay Dilger, Senior Specialist in American National Government, rdilger@crs.loc.gov, 7-3110, and Sean Lowry, Analyst in Public Finance, slowry@crs.loc.gov, 7-9154. For a more detailed discussion, see CRS Report R42695, SBA Veterans Assistance Programs: An Analysis of Contemporary Issues, by Robert Jay Dilger and Sean Lowry.

[45] U.S. Congress, Senate Committee on Banking and Currency, Extension of the Small Business Act of 1953, report to accompany S. 2127, 84th Cong., 1st sess., July 22, 1955, S.Rept. 84-1350 (Washington: GPO, 1955), p. 17.

[46] U.S. Small Business Administration (SBA), "FY2016 Congressional Budget Justification and FY2014 Annual Performance Report," pp. 97-101, at https://www.sba.gov /sites/default/ files/1- FY%202016%20CBJ%20FY%202014%20APR.PDF.

[47] SBA, "Operation Boots to Business: From Service to Startup," at https://www.sba. gov/offices/headquarters/ovbd/resources/160511; and SBA, "Operation Boots to Business: Fact Sheet," at https://www.sba.gov/sites/default/files/files/B2B_Fact%20Sheet.pdf.

[48] SBA, "SBA Sets Fees on New Loans Under $150,000 to Zero, Getting Loans Into the Hands of More Entrepreneurs," October 30, 2013, at https://www.sba.gov/blogs/sba-sets-fees-new-loans-under-150000-zero-gettingloans-hands-more-entrepreneurs.

[49] SBA, "SBA Announces New Measures to Help Get Small Business Loans Into the Hands of Veterans," November 8, 2013, at https://www.sba.gov/content/sba-announces-new-measures-help-get-small-business-loans-hands-veterans; and U.S. Small Business Administration, "Procedural Notice: SBA Veterans Advantage," December 18, 2013, at https://www.sba.gov/sites/default/files/lender_notices/5000-1299_0.pdf.

[50] Ibid.

[51] SBA, "The SBA Express Pilot Program: Inspection Report," June 1998, p. 3.

[52] SBA, "FY2016 Congressional Budget Justification and FY2014 Annual Performance Report," pp. 10, 38, 39, 93, at https://www.sba.gov/sites/default/files/1-FY%202016%20CBJ% 20FY%202014%20APR.PDF. Legislation was introduced during the 113th Congress (S. 2143, the Veterans Entrepreneurship Act) to make the veteran SBAExpress fee waiver permanent. P.L. 113-235, the Consolidated and Further Continuing Appropriations Act, 2015, provided statutory authorization for the veteran SBAExpress fee waiver for FY2015.

[53] SBA, "Disaster Assistance Program: SOP 50-30-7," May 13, 2011, p. 48, at https://www. sba.gov/sites/default/files/sops/SOP%2050%2030%207.pdf; and 13 C.F.R. §123.508. For further information and analysis concerning the SBA's disaster assistance loan program, see CRS Report R41309, The SBA Disaster Loan Program: Overview and Possible Issues for Congress, by Bruce R. Lindsay.

[54] See CRS Report RL33243, Small Business Administration: A Primer on Programs and Funding, by Robert Jay Dilger and Sean Lowry.

[55] See P.L. 100-656, the Business Opportunity Development Reform Act of 1988 and P.L. 105-135, the HUBZone Act of 1997—Title VI of the Small Business Reauthorization Act of 1997 (small businesses generally); and P.L. 106-50, the Veterans Entrepreneurship and Small Business Development Act of 1999 (service-disabled-veteran-owned).

[56] For more information on the VR&E program, see CRS Report RL34627, Veterans' Benefits: The Vocational Rehabilitation and Employment Program, by Benjamin Collins.

[57] VR&E also provides independent living services to veterans who are not able to work. In FY2013, approximately 20% of completed rehabilitations under VR&E were independent living (i.e., not employment-based) rehabilitations.

[58] FY2015 estimates are on page VBA-84 and VBA-251 of Volume III of the FY2016 VA budget, available at http://www.va.gov/budget/docs/summary/Fy2016-VolumeIIIBenefits BurialProgramsAndDeptmentalAdministration.pdf.

[59] This section was prepared by David H. Bradley, Specialist in Labor Economics, dbradley@crs.loc.gov, 7-7352.

[60] While non-disabled veterans with barriers to employment may receive direct services from DVOP personnel, statute specifies that veterans with service-connected disabilities receive the highest priority of service. See 38 U.S.C. 4103A.

[61] JVSG is described in greater detail in the "Jobs for Veterans State Grants" section of this report. More information on veteran-related initiatives administered the U.S. Department of Labor, including the JVSG program, is available at http://www.dol.gov/vets/.

[62] For more information on the "30% or More Disabled Veterans" hiring authority, see http://www.opm.gov/staffingportal/vetguide.asp#30%Disabled.

[63] For more information on the HVRP, see CRS Report RL34024, Veterans and Homelessness, by Libby Perl.

[64] For more information on TRIO programs, including Upward Bound, see CRS Report R42724, The TRIO Programs: A Primer, by Cassandria Dortch.

[65] U.S. Department of Education, Veterans Upward Bound Program, Funding Status, http://www2.ed.gov/programs/triovub/funding.html, as downloaded on January 5, 2014.

[66] For more information on the WOTC, see CRS Report R43729, The Work Opportunity Tax Credit, by Benjamin Collins and Sarah A. Donovan. This report also describes nonveteran target populations that are eligible for the WOTC (e.g., at-risk youth or individuals convicted of a felony).

[67] The size of the WOTC was based on wages paid the employee during the first year of employment. In cases where an eligible hire worked between 120 and 400 hours, the tax credit was reduced to 25% of wages paid. If the eligible hire worked fewer than 120 hours, the employer was not eligible for the credit.

[68] For example, authorization for the WOTC lapsed after December 31, 2013, but was retroactively authorized for 2014 by the Tax Increase Prevention Act of 2014 (P.L. 113-295), which was enacted in December 2014. For more information on Tax Extenders for 2014, see CRS Report R43898, Tax Provisions that Expired in 2014 ("Tax Extenders"), by Molly F. Sherlock

[69] See "WOTC Program Guidance," http://www.doleta.gov/business/incentives/opptax/pdf/ InterimInstructions_2014Reauthorization_2015Hiatus.pdf.

In: Support for Servicemembers and Veterans ISBN: 978-1-63484-950-0
Editor: Gayle Marsh

Chapter 3

VETERANS' BENEFITS: THE VOCATIONAL REHABILITATION AND EMPLOYMENT PROGRAM*

Benjamin Collins

SUMMARY

Vocational Rehabilitation and Employment for veterans (VR&E) is an entitlement program that provides job training and other employment-related services to veterans with service-connected disabilities. In cases where a disabled veteran is not able to work, the VR&E program provides independent living (IL) services to help the veteran achieve the highest possible quality of life. The VR&E program is administered by the Veterans Benefits Administration (VBA), part of the Department of Veterans Affairs (VA).

To be entitled to VR&E services, a veteran must have been discharged under conditions other than dishonorable and be found to have either (1) a 20% service-connected disability and an employment handicap, or (2) a 10% service-connected disability and a serious employment handicap. After a veteran is found to be entitled to VR&E, a counselor helps the veteran identify a suitable employment goal and determine what services

* This is an edited, reformatted and augmented version of a Congressional Research Service publication RL34627, prepared for Members and Committees of Congress, dated January 20, 2015.

will be necessary to achieve that goal. The veteran is then assigned to one of five reemployment tracks:

- Reemployment for veterans who wish to return to work they held prior to their military service;
- Rapid Access to Employment for veterans who already have the skills necessary to compete in the job market and only need short-term services such as job search assistance;
- Employment through Long-Term Services for veterans who require postsecondary or vocational training to reach their employment goals;
- Self-employment for veterans who have the skills to start businesses; or
- Independent Living for veterans for whom employment is not a viable goal.

Veterans may change tracks if a disability worsens or if their employment objective changes. Services may be provided by the VA, though they are more frequently purchased from an outside provider.
VR&E benefits are typically limited to 48 months, though the benefit period can be extended under certain circumstances. In most cases, veterans are entitled to a subsistence allowance while they are enrolled in an education or training program.
In FY2013, approximately 34,800 veterans developed a new plan of service with VR&E and almost 10,400 veterans completed rehabilitation.
In FY2013, costs for mandatory VR&E benefits were approximately $931 million. Discretionary support services and other administrative costs were approximately $187 million.

Vocational Rehabilitation and Employment for veterans (VR&E) is an entitlement program that provides job training and related services "to enable veterans with service-connected disabilities to achieve maximum independence in daily living and, to the maximum extent feasible, to become employable and to obtain and maintain suitable employment."[1] The program is administered by the Department of Veterans Affairs (VA). The VR&E program provides comprehensive services to enable veterans with service-connected disabilities and employment handicaps to become employable and maintain suitable employment.[2] For severely disabled veterans for whom employment is not possible, the program strives to help them achieve the highest quality of independent living possible with a future chance of employment, given medical and technological advances.

This report provides an overview of the VR&E program. After a brief background section, it describes how the program establishes individual veterans' entitlements and the scope of benefits and services available to qualified veterans. The final section provides participation and outcome data.

BACKGROUND

History

In 1918, Congress passed P.L. 65-178, the Vocational Rehabilitation Act, to provide for the retraining of disabled persons who served in the U.S. military and naval forces. The rehabilitation program was administered by the Federal Board for Vocational Education. On August 24, 1921, control of veterans' rehabilitation was transferred to the newly created Veterans' Bureau. In 1930, Congress created the Veterans Administration by combining three bureaus: the Veterans' Bureau, the Bureau of Pensions, and the National Homes for Disabled Volunteer Veterans. In 1943, Congress passed P.L. 78-16, which broadened eligibility and provided that any eligible veteran may receive up to four years of training specifically directed to restoring employability.

In subsequent years, the scope of the veterans' rehabilitation program has been modified and expanded to better fulfill its mission. The program has undergone several name changes and has usually been housed with the education services in the Department of Veterans' Affairs (VA). In 1999, the VR&E program acquired its current name with the intention of emphasizing employment services and job placement.

In 2004, the Secretary of Veterans Affairs responded to continuing criticisms of VR&E's operations from congressional committees, the Government Accountability Office, and others by forming a task force to evaluate the program. The task force report found little evidence that the program's efforts to obtain jobs for rehabilitated veterans had been effective.[3] Among its 110 recommendations, the task force emphasized that VR&E should focus on employment and place more emphasis on its clients' skills rather than their disabilities. In response to these recommendations, VR&E developed the five-track employment process discussed later in this report.[4]

Authorization and Administration

The VR&E program is authorized by Chapter 31 of Title 38 of the U.S. Code. Veterans' benefits are often referred to by their authorizing chapter of Title 38. As such, VR&E benefits are often described as "Chapter 31" benefits.[5] The VR&E program is administered by the Veterans Benefits Administration (VBA) within the VA.

Financing and Costs

VR&E costs are divided between mandatory and discretionary spending. VR&E funds are appropriated with other VA-administered readjustment benefits in the Military Construction-Veterans Affairs appropriations bill.

VR&E benefits and the subsistence allowances for VR&E beneficiaries are mandatory spending. Costs for these activities in FY2013 were $931 million. This total consists of $564 million for VR&E benefits in the form of tuition, books, and other direct assistance as well as $367 million in subsistence allowances for individuals who were enrolled in an eligible training program.[6] *Table 1* presents benefit costs from FY2009 through FY2013.

Table 1. Vocational Rehabilitation and Employment Program Benefit Costs, FY2009-FY2013

(nominal dollars in millions)

	FY2009	FY2010	FY2011	FY2012	FY2013
Tuition, Books, Supplies, etc.	$447	$463	$472	$489	$564
Subsistence Allowance	$276	$297	$287	$302	$367
Total	$723	$760	$759	$791	$931

Source: Department of Veterans Affairs Budget Justifications, FY2011 through FY2015, available at http://www.va.gov/budget/products.asp.

Notes: Table reflects actual costs for mandatory benefits. Costs do not include administrative expenses and other discretionary services.

The VR&E program's discretionary costs, which cover VR&E staff, counseling from such staff, and other expenses, were $187 million for FY2013. In FY2013, the VR&E program reported that it employed 1,502 full-time equivalents.[7]

VR&E APPLICATION PROCESS

There are two determinations between a veteran's application for VR&E and his or her receipt of services: *eligibility* and *entitlement*.

Eligibility

A veteran must apply to the VA to establish eligibility. To be eligible for VR&E services, a veteran must[8]

- have served on or after September 16, 1940;
- have received, or will receive, a discharge under conditions other than dishonorable;[9] and
- have a service-connected disability rating of 10% or greater.[10]

Active duty service members are eligible for VR&E services if their service-connected disabilities are reasonably expected to be rated at a minimum of at least 20% following their discharge.

Duration of Eligibility

Veterans are eligible for VR&E services for 12 years after separation from active military duty. In cases where a veteran was notified of a service-connected disability rating after separation, eligibility extends 12 years from the date of notification.

The period of eligibility may be extended if the VA determines that the veteran has a serious employment handicap, has not yet been rehabilitated to the point of employability, has been rehabilitated but still cannot perform the duties required, or needs more services because the occupational requirements have changed. An objective evaluation is required for these circumstances to be determined.[11]

For independent living services, if the medical condition is so severe that achievement of the vocational goal is not feasible and that goal is necessary to ensure that the veteran will achieve maximum independence, the period of eligibility may be extended.[12]

Entitlement

Once eligibility is established, an applicant completes a comprehensive evaluation with a Vocational Rehabilitation Counselor (VRC). The evaluation includes

- an assessment of the veteran's interests, aptitudes, and abilities;
- an assessment of whether service-connected disabilities impair the veteran's ability to secure and maintain suitable employment; and
- identification of services necessary to maintain a career or achieve maximum independence.

An applicant is entitled to VR&E services if the evaluation finds that he or she has

- a 20% service-connected disability and an employment handicap; or
- a 10% service-connected disability and a serious employment handicap.

An *employment handicap* is an impairment of a veteran's ability to prepare for, obtain, or retain employment consistent with his or her abilities, aptitudes, and interests.[13]

A *serious employment handicap* is a significant impairment of a veteran's ability to prepare for, obtain, or retain employment consistent with his or her abilities, aptitudes, and interests.[14]

To be entitled to VR&E services, the veteran's service-connected disability must contribute to the employment handicap and VR&E must be able to identify, observe, and measure it.

Non-entitlement

A veteran who applies for VR&E services but is not found to be entitled to services is to be informed about appeal rights and the appeals process. The VA will also use the information gathered in the application process to recommend other services.[15]

CASE MANAGEMENT AND REHABILITATION PLANNING

After a veteran is found to be entitled to VR&E services, a case manager is assigned to work with the veteran. The case manager works in conjunction with a VRC and the veteran to determine an employment goal and assess obstacles to employment. A written rehabilitation plan is then developed, describing the goal of the VR&E program and the services required to achieve the goal.[16] The required services may be provided by the VRC or the case manager may provide referrals for other services. The plan is reviewed with the participation of the client at least once a year.[17]

SERVICES PROVIDED BY VR&E

The most common services provided by VR&E agencies are funding for higher education and short-term employment services like job search assistance. The full range of services that VR&E agencies are required to make available to entitled clients, however, is much broader and includes a variety of specialized services for workers with disabilities.[18]

Service Delivery Tracks

Each VR&E beneficiary is assigned to a service delivery track based on the veteran's objective and services needed. If necessary, a veteran may change tracks while enrolled in the VR&E program.

Reemployment Track

The Reemployment Track is for veterans who wish to return to work with their previous employers. In addition to the case management and counseling that all VR&E beneficiaries receive, veterans on the reemployment track may receive assistance from the VA to make their workplace more accessible. They may also receive counseling on workplace rights for veterans.[19]

A veteran on this track is considered rehabilitated when he or she has completed the employment program and maintained suitable employment for 60 days.[20]

Rapid Access to Employment Track

The Rapid Access to Employment Track emphasizes the goal of immediate employment and is available to separating veterans who already have the skills necessary to compete in the job market in suitable occupations. On this track, VR&E services may include job readiness preparation, resume development, or job search assistance. The VRC may also counsel veterans on this track in disability rights and assist an employer in providing accommodations to a disability.

A veteran on this track is considered rehabilitated when he or she has completed the employment program and maintained suitable employment for 60 days.

Self-Employment Track

This track is for veterans who have limited access to traditional employment and need flexible work schedules and a more accommodating work environment because of their disabling conditions or other special circumstances. Veterans may be provided with assistance in the development of a business plan, training in the operation of small businesses, financial assistance, and guidance on obtaining adequate resources to implement the business plan.

A veteran on this track is considered rehabilitated when he or she has completed the self-employment program and maintained a viable business for one year.

Employment through Long-Term Services Track

This track targets veterans who need long-term employment training to prepare them for suitable employment. Formal classroom courses are the most common long-term service, though training may also include on-the-job training, apprenticeships, internships, or other workplace preparation programs.

Services last as long as is necessary for the beneficiary to attain the objectives set out in his or her employment plan, but may not exceed 48 months (or the equivalent when pursued on a part-time basis).[21] In limited circumstances (such as a veteran's disability worsening during the rehabilitation process and the original employment objective becoming unviable), a rehabilitation program can be extended beyond 48 months. Extensions must be approved by a counseling psychologist and a VR&E officer.[22]

A veteran on the employment through long-term services track is considered rehabilitated when he or she has completed a training program and maintained employment for 60 days.

Independent Living Services Track

The Independent Living (IL) Services Track is for veterans who may not be able to work immediately and need additional rehabilitation to enable them to live more independently. The short-term focus of the program is on allowing veterans to participate in family and community life, but it also aims to increase their ability to possibly return to work in the longer term.[23] Veterans on this VR&E track may be provided with assistive technology, independent living skills training, and connections to community-based support services.

Unlike the other VR&E tracks, the IL track is limited in the number of veterans it can serve. Currently, 2,700 veterans are permitted to begin an IL program each year.[24] This limit is waived for veterans who have been adversely affected by a natural or other disaster, as determined by the VA.[25]

To meet the needs of veterans with severe disabilities and mobility impairments, VR&E's IL program may work with the VA's Loan Guaranty Service and the Specially Adapted Housing (SAH) grant program, the Home Improvements and Structural Alterations (HISA) program, the Automobile Adaptive Equipment program, and the Visually Impaired Services Team (VIST).[26] The VR&E also works with the Committee on Care of Veterans with Severe Mental Illness (SMI)[27] and the Traumatic Brain Injury Caregivers Panel.[28]

IL programs for veterans are typically limited to 24 months. This limit can be extended if the VA determines that an extension would substantially increase a veteran's level of independence in daily living. The limit may also be extended for veterans who served after September 11, 2011, and have a severe disability.

Monetary Benefits for VR&E Participants

In addition to training benefits and other employment services, veterans who are entitled to VR&E services are also eligible for certain financial benefits.

Subsistence Allowance

Many veterans who are receiving benefits under the VR&E program are also eligible for a monthly subsistence allowance. Veterans who are only receiving (1) initial evaluation, (2) placement or post-placement services, and (3) counseling from the VR&E program are not eligible for a subsistence allowance, nor are veterans who are enrolled in a training program less than half-time.[29]

The VR&E subsistence allowance varies by the type of program the veteran is enrolled in and whether or not the veteran has dependents. As of October 1, 2014, the monthly allowance for a veteran enrolled full-time at an institute of higher learning with two dependents is $882.[30] The subsistence allowance is increased each year proportionate to the rate of inflation.[31] The subsistence allowance continues as long as the veteran is enrolled in an eligible program and continues for two months after the program of training has been completed. In cases where a veteran is displaced as the result of a natural or other disaster while receiving a subsistence allowance, the subsistence allowance is extended for an additional two months.[32]

Typically, veterans are not permitted to participate in both the VR&E program and another VA educational program (such as a G.I. Bill program). However, veterans who are eligible for both VR&E services and the Post-9/11 GI Bill (also known as Chapter 33 benefits) may collect the housing allowance offered under Chapter 33 while receiving training and other benefits under VR&E. This policy was instituted to eliminate the incentive for disabled veterans to choose the Post-9/11 G.I. Bill (which typically offers a higher cash allowance but fewer services) over the VR&E program (which offers a lower cash allowance but more supportive services).

Unlike the VR&E subsistence allowances, which are the same for veterans nationwide, Chapter 33 housing allowances are determined by a veteran's geographic location. In many cases, Chapter 33 housing allowances are greater than VR&E subsistence allowances: as of October 1, 2014, the Chapter 33 housing allowance ranges from about $840 to about $3,700 per month.[33]

In FY2013, the VA reported that VR&E subsistence allowance benefits totaled $367 million.[34] This estimate includes VR&E beneficiaries who collected the traditional subsistence allowance as well as VR&E beneficiaries who collected the Chapter 33 housing allowances in place of the VR&E subsistence allowance.

VR&E Loans

Veterans who are entitled to VR&E benefits may also be eligible for interest-free loans. These loans are only available to veterans who have a plan of service with VR&E and "would otherwise be unable to begin, continue or reenter his or her rehabilitation program."[35] The maximum loan amount is equal to twice the weekly subsistence allowance for a veteran with no dependents ($1,207 in FY2014).[36]

Repayment of the loan is made in monthly installments from future wages, pensions, subsistence allowances, educational assistance allowance, or retirement pay. The VA reported that 2,693 loans totaling approximately $2.4 million were made in FY2013 and that the default rate was less than 0.5%.[37] The VR&E loan program cost $453,000 in FY2013, of which $346,000 was for administrative expenses.[38]

VR&E Participation and Outcome Data

Table 2 shows participation data from FY2008 through FY2013. The categories for "applicants," "eligible," "completed evaluation," "entitled to services," and "new plans of service" trace the number of individuals who continued through each stage of the application process, and in many cases, a single veteran may be counted in multiple categories. The "rehabilitated" category includes veterans who secured and maintained suitable employment or completed an independent living program.

Table 2. Vocational Rehabilitation & Employment Program Statistics, FY2008-FY2013

VR&E Category	2008	2009	2010	2011	2012	2013
Applicants	68,949	77,998	69,390	65,239	72,605	80,812
Eligible	65,784	74,617	66,717	62,726	69,683	78,159
Completed evaluation	39,910	44,089	46,523	n/a	61,622	66,749
Entitled to Services	35,166	38,802	41,102	41,229	45,167	54,440
New Plans of Service	26,703	28,997	27,904	27,821	30,806	34,806
Rehabilitated	11,039	11,022	10,038	9,862	9,949	10,397
Participants	103,126	110,750	117,130	116,295	121,236	135,815

Source: Table prepared by CRS using data from the Department of Veterans Affairs, Veterans Benefits Administration, Annual Benefits Report for FY2008-FY2013. Reports are available at http://www.vba.va.gov/REPORTS/abr/index.asp.

"Participants" include veterans in any stage of the VR&E process after the applicant and evaluation phases have been completed. In includes veterans who began a VR&E plan in a prior year as well as those in interrupted rehabilitation plan status.

Due to the multi-year nature of many rehabilitations and the complex and diverse nature of the VR&E population, the data in *Table 2* should not be used to calculate the efficacy of the program. A more precise indicator of efficacy may be the VR&E rehabilitation rate, which is published by the VA each year. In calculating this rate, the numerator is the total number of rehabilitated veterans and the denominator is the total number of veterans exiting the program minus veterans who are employed in jobs other than their rehabilitation objective, are unemployable for medical or psychological reasons, or transferred to the Post-9/11 GI Bill program. In FY2013, VR&E's rehabilitation rate was 68%. Between FY2010 and FY2012, the rate varied between 76% and 77%.[39]

Table 3 shows the types of programs that beneficiaries participated in during FY2013. The table only includes individuals who were concurrently receiving a subsistence allowance while they completed an educational program. It does not include individuals who were receiving training without an accompanying subsistence allowance nor does it include individuals who received nonmonetary benefits from VR&E such as counseling or job search assistance.

Table 3. Training Programs of VR&E Beneficiaries, FY2013

Program	Individuals	Share of Beneficiaries
Undergraduate School	53,780	79.8%
Graduate School	5,849	8.7%
Vocational/Technical School	3,486	5.2%
College, Non-degree	1,635	2.4%
Othera	2,683	4.0%
Total	67,433	100.0%

Source: Department of Veterans Affairs, Veterans Benefits Administration Annual Benefits Report for FY2013, VR&E Section, p.7. http://www.benefits.va.gov/REPORTS/abr/ABR-VocRehab-FY13-09262014.pdf.

Note: Data only include individuals who received a subsistence allowance.

[a] Includes veterans enrolled in extended evaluation, independent living, paid on-the job training, non-pay work experience in government, non-paid on the job training, apprenticeships, improvement of rehabilitation potential, high school, or a farm co-op.

Table 4 presents more detail on VR&E participants who completed the rehabilitation process in FY2013. About 84% of veterans who were rehabilitated achieved an employment outcome. Among rehabilitated veterans who achieved an employment outcome, the average annual wage after rehabilitation was $37,717.[40]

Table 4. Outcomes for Veterans Rehabilitated Through the VR&E Program, FY2013

	Number	Share of Rehabilitated VR&E Participants
Rehabilitated VR&E Participants	10,397	100.0%
Completed Independent Living Program	1,708	16.4%
Achieved Employment Outcome	8,689	83.6%

Source: Department of Veterans Affairs, Veterans Benefits Administration Annual Benefits Report for FY2013, VR&E Section, p.10 and 11. http://www.benefits.va.gov/REPORTS/abr/ABR-VocRehab-FY13-09262014.pdf.

End Notes

[1] See 38 U.S.C. 3100.

[2] The VBA website defines suitable employment as "Employment that does not aggravate the Veteran's disabilities, is stable, and is consistent with his or her pattern of abilities, aptitudes, and interests." See http://www.vba.va.gov/bln/vre/def.htm#se.

[3] Department of Veterans Affairs, VA Vocational Rehabilitation and Employment Task Force, Report to the Secretary of Veterans Affairs: The Vocational Rehabilitation and Employment Program for the 21st Century Veteran, 2004.

[4] Testimony of Ruth Fanning, Director, VA's VR&E Service, before the Senate Committee on Veterans' Affairs, February 5, 2008, available at http://www.va.gov/OCA/testimony/svac/080205RF.asp.

[5] Other examples include the Post-9/11 G.I. Bill (Chapter 33) and the Montgomery G.I. Bill-Active Duty (Chapter 30).

[6] Department of Veterans Affairs FY2015 Budget, Volume III: Benefits and Burial Programs and Departmental Administration, page VBA-32, http://www.va.gov/budget/products.asp.

[7] Department of Veterans Affairs FY2015 Budget, Volume III: Benefits and Burial Programs and Departmental Administration, page VBA-249, http://www.va.gov/budget/products.asp.

[8] See 38 U.S.C. 3102-3103.

[9] For more information on discharge criteria, see CRS Report R42324, "Who is a Veteran?"—Basic Eligibility for Veterans' Benefits, by Umar Moulta-Ali.

[10] For an in-depth discussion of the VA's disability evaluation process and policies, see archived CRS Report RL33991, Disability Evaluation of Military Servicemembers, by Christine Scott and Don J. Jansen.

[11] See 38 U.S.C. 3013(c).

[12] See 38 U.S.C. 3103(d).

[13] See 38 U.S.C. 3101(1).

[14] See 38 U.S.C. 3101(2).

[15] For more information on federal employment programs for veterans, see CRS Report R42790, Employment for Veterans: Trends and Programs, coordinated by Benjamin Collins.

[16] See 38 U.S.C. 3106.

[17] See 38 U.S.C. 3106(b).

[18] Additional required services may include corrective assistive devices, travel expenses, and independent living services. See 38 U.S.C. 3104, 3109, and 3120.

[19] In addition to the rights afforded by the Americans with Disabilities Act of 1990 (ADA; 42 U.S.C. 12101-12213), disabled veterans are also entitled to additional rights under the Uniformed Services Employment and Reemployment Rights Act of 1994 (USERRA, 38 U.S.C. 4301-4335).

[20] Rehabilitation criteria are from the Government Accountability Office (GAO) report VA Vocational Rehabilitation and Employment: Better Incentives, Workforce Planning, and Performance Reporting Could Improve Program. January 2009. Rehabilitation criteria are also available at 38 C.F.R. 21.283.

[21] See 38 C.F.R. 21.70(b)(1).

[22] See 38 C.F.R. 21.78.

[23] See 38 U.S.C. 3109.

[24] This limit of 2,700 was established by the Veterans Benefits Act of 2010 (P.L. 111-275). The cap was previously increased to 2,500 by the Veterans Education and Benefits Expansion Act of 2001 (P.L. 107-103) and to 2,600 by the Veterans' Benefits Improvement Act of 2008 (P.L. 110-389).

[25] See 38 U.S.C. 3120(e)(2). This change was made by Section 701(c) of P.L. 112-154, Honoring America's Veterans and Caring for Camp Lejeune Families Act of 2012.

[26] For information on housing and automobile grants, see CRS Report RL34626, Veterans' Benefits: Disabled Veterans.

[27] The 2004 VR&E Task Force Report noted "that the single largest group of veterans for whom an employment plan is not considered feasible was for veterans with psychiatric disabilities," p. A-64.

[28] P.L. 110-181, signed by President George W. Bush on January 28, 2008, mandated the creation of the Traumatic Brain Injury Caregivers Panel to develop coordinated, uniform, and consistent training curricula to be used in training family members in the provision of care and assistance to current and former members of the Armed Forces with traumatic brain injury. For details, see CRS Report RL34371, "Wounded Warrior" and Veterans Provisions in the FY2008 National Defense Authorization Act, by Sarah A. Lister, Christine Scott, and Sidath Viranga Panangala.

[29] See 38 U.S.C. 3108 and 38 C.F.R. 21.260(d).

[30] A complete list of subsistence rates for VR&E participants as of October 1, 2014, is available at http://www.benefits.va.gov/VOCREHAB/docs/SAFY15.pdf.

[31] See 38 U.S.C. 3108.

[32] See 38 U.S.C. 3108(a)(2)(B). This change was made by Section 701(b) of P.L. 112-154, Honoring America's Veterans and Caring for Camp Lejeune Families Act of 2012.

[33] The allowance under Chapter 33 is equal to the basic housing allowance for a service member with dependents in pay grade E-5. Allowances are determined by zip code. Full list of allowances by locality are at http://www.defensetravel.dod.mil/Docs/perdiem/browse/Allowances/BAH/PDF/2014/2014-With-Dependents-BAHRates.pdf

http://www.defensetravel.dod.mil/Docs/perdiem/browse/Allowances/BAH/PDF/2013/2013-With-Dependents-BAH-Rates.pdf.

[34] U.S. Department of Veterans Affairs, FY2015 Budget Submission, Volume III: Benefits and Burial Programs and Departmental Administration, page VBA-32, http://www.va.gov/budget/products.asp.

[35] See 38 C.F.R. 21.274(c).

[36] See 38 U.S.C. 3112.

[37] U.S. Department of Veterans Affairs, FY2015 Budget Submission, Volume III: Benefits and Burial Programs and Departmental Administration, page VBA-61, http://www.va.gov/budget/products.asp.

[38] U.S. Department of Veterans Affairs, FY2015 Budget Submission, Volume III: Benefits and Burial Programs and Departmental Administration, page VBA-61, http://www.va.gov/budget/products.asp.

[39] U.S. Department of Veterans Affairs, FY2015 Budget Submission, Volume III: Benefits and Burial Programs and Departmental Administration, page VBA-260, http://www.va.gov/budget/products.asp.

[40] Department of Veterans Affairs, Veterans Benefits Administration Annual Benefits Report for FY2013, VR&E Section, p. 11. http://www.benefits.va.gov/REPORTS/abr/ABR-VocRehab-FY13-09262014.pdf.

INDEX

#

A

B

C

D

E

J

L

M

N

O

P

Q

R

S